bring the

FEAST

The Pilgrim Press
Cleveland, Ohio

bring the

fEAST

songs

from the re-imagining

community

The Pilgrim Press, Cleveland, Ohio 44115

© 1998 The Pilgrim Press
Illustrations © 1998 by Nancy Chinn

contents

introduction

Re-imagining music in the life of the church? Yes! Women and men are making significant contributions of new sounds and images to celebrate life in the Spirit of Christ. This renewal is ongoing but has been especially explosive in the second half of the twentieth century. The plethora of new denominational hymnals and supplementary resources available for the contemporary church make exciting but challenging work for the church musician when examining new materials.

The Re-Imagining Community has gathered this collection to celebrate and highlight commissioned works within the Re-Imagining Community and its conferences since 1993. We have also integrated music representing the global community. In this collection we especially, though not exclusively, lift up the work of women. As has been true historically, much of this music originated in a specific community for a particular occasion, but has since taken on a life of its own as it has been shared from one community to another. By singing songs from neighboring communities and varied cultures, our God expands and we stand in solidarity with people of faith throughout the world.

In creating *Bring the Feast,* our hope is to offer a supplemental music resource that will serve the Christian community in experiencing and integrating the voice of the feminine—Divine and incarnated. We foresee these materials to be of use in local congregations, conferences, and small worship gatherings.

The editorial committee for *Bring the Feast* was guided by the following considerations:

- Artistic voices speak, for the most part, in images and metaphor rather than in concepts.
- Teachings of music and poetry widen theological discourse.
- Renewed emphasis on healing within the Christian community calls for appropriate songs of healing.
- Spirit is invoked in new and mysterious ways.
- The affective languages of music and movement are strengthened when performed together.

A committee of four people guided the compilation process over a period of a year. We met with regularity, played and sang hundreds of songs, and studied copyright law. Midway through the process we invited in a group from the Re-Imagining Community to listen to the music we had found and to share their responses with us. Joan Prefontaine served as our primary guide on matters poetic. Donna Kasbohm, offering years of experience as a church musician, provided keen musical ears. Jane Ramseyer Miller kept us aware of the many global and cross-cultural possibilities in our selection process. Madelin Sue Martin served as convener, musical editor, and primary writer of the performance notes. These women all live and work in Minnesota, where the "women are strong," as Garrison Keillor reminds us weekly, and where Re-Imagining keeps its home base.

Each song is interlined with music chosen for the particular text. Because many of the lyrical pieces may also stand alone as poetry, we have presented the texts in poetic form for further reflection. Piano accompaniment, descants, harmony, and rhythm parts are included with the congregational presentation of selected songs. The commentary section provides performance suggestions for each composition as well as background on the origin or context from which the materials emerged. Finally, we have included several indexes that should prove useful to worship planners and anyone seeking to locate a work more quickly.

We thank the Re-Imagining Community for its ongoing support of this project. We are grateful for financial contributions which supported this work through a generous grant from the Faith, Hope and Love Foundation in Minnesota. We thank all the wordsmiths and music makers for their contributions. SophiaSpirit receives our gratitude for her inspiration and for calling us to dream unabashedly in new ways. Our deepest appreciation goes finally to the small band of women who gave vision, shape, and countless hours to bring this book to birth.

madelin sue martin

Re-Imagining is a global, ecumenical community of acceptance where exploration, discussion, study, and practice of the Christian faith are carried out freely and responsibly to seek justice, honor creation, and call the church into solidarity with all people of God.

Address correspondence to:
　　The Re-Imagining Community
　　122 West Franklin Avenue, Room 4A
　　Minneapolis, Minnesota 55404-2470
　　(612) 879-8036; (612) 879-8464, fax

Notes on the songs

1 A PROPHET-WOMAN BROKE A JAR

This text was commissioned for a Presbyterian church in Thunder Bay, Ontario. It retells the story of two important biblical women—the woman with the jar of rare nard, who anoints Jesus, and Mary at the tomb, who announces the resurrection. The hymn can serve in any setting where the strength of relationships is celebrated. In addition to its use in a strophic format, it is also possible to extract an antiphon for calling the Spirit by using the last two lines of the text or some other combination of two lines. The music from the first full phrase works with the last full phrase, which is the same except for the cadence note. This lilting response might be accompanied by sounds of the Spirit's breath or a drone bass F using the words "Spirit calling" in half-note rhythm.

2 BLESS NOW, O GOD, THE JOURNEY ("HYMN OF COVENANT")

Madelin Sue Martin writes: "This hymn was used at the 1993 Re-Imagining Conference as a thanksgiving following the milk and honey ritual. The text from Sylvia Dunstan's collection *In Search of Hope and Grace* caught our attention early in the planning, but seemed in search of a tune. At the same time, we wanted to use the tune HOLY MANNA for a circle table dance." This new setting was composed as a companion in both style and key to HOLY MANNA by Martin, ritual coordinator for the conference. Sylvia Dunstan was a United Church of Canada minister, now deceased following a bout with cancer. Two volumes of her hymn texts are published by G.I.A. Publications, Inc., in Chicago, Illinois.

3 BLESS SOPHIA

This chant was developed from the memory of a song from the Merry Monarch Festival in Hilo, Hawaii. David Haas put the three phrases of ritual text together. The Re-Imagining Community first sang this haunting blessing beginning in 1991 during the two years of planning for the 1993 conference, and continues to sing it frequently. In keeping with Hawaiian simplicity, this piece is best accompanied only by an ipu, the Hawaiian gourd drum. The pattern is "long-short-short" through-out. It is effective to raise the key by half steps each time if singing it repeatedly.

4   Blessed Are the Persecuted (Sean benditos los que sufren)

This oral-tradition piece picks up some of the language of the Beatitudes and asserts that the Spirit lives within those who seek the Christ. It has been brought to the table by the Mennonite World Conference. This rhythmic, syncopated, triadic music may be accompanied by rhythm instruments and/or hand-clapping. The equal-voice style lends itself well to many configurations. If using it with an SATB choir, alternate between men's and women's voices, and then have six parts when all are singing. Although strophic in form, teach this piece by memory, not from the book.

5   Braided Rugs ("Braided Lives")

Composer Jane Ramseyer Miller writes: "'Braided Lives' was written for my dear neighbor and friend Mark Molina, who died of a brain tumor at six years of age. In the months before his death, our congregation gathered nearly weekly at his home to be with Mark and sing his favorite songs. The mixture of singing, laughter, and weeping during those months was an experience I cherish. As we sang with Mark, we began to weave a braided rug made from scraps of Mark's clothes and from the closets of each member of our community. When he died, 'Braided Lives' was sung at his funeral. His rug has found its place at the center of our worship space, where the children sit for stories and activities."

This piece is well served by guitar or piano accompaniment and a solo instrument like a flute or recorder. In a healing-service context, this text draws out the communal connections of prayer for and prayer with others who are in need of healing. The last two phrases could be used as a mantra under spontaneous spoken prayer by the community. This piece cries out for the ritual action of laying on of hands or anointing with oil as possible symbolic gestures.

6   Bring Many Names

The music was composed for the 1993 Re-Imagining Conference and served as part of the gathering rite on the opening evening. The hymn could be sung at any worship service as a gathering piece. A full choral concertato published by World Library Publications gives a much richer musical rendering with instrumental obbligatos, choir parts, descants, and alternate accompaniments. There is much musical mix-and-match possibility here for music directors.

7   Bring the Feast to Every Hillside

In 1996, Christine Smith commissioned this poem to honor her preaching theme for the Florida UCC Ministerial Conference. It was later used as a theme song for "Dancing at the Table," a conference of Mennonite and Church of the Brethren congregations that welcome gay and lesbian members. This is a true hymn of the Word in its proclamation and response to both the biblical Word and the preached Word. From the beginning, Joan Prefontaine worked with the sturdy and familiar early American tune NETTLETON. Jane Miller later wrote this very convincing music with a syncopated measure as its signature. Singers are encouraged to use the piece in its entirety in order to be faithful to the message. Interludes of eight bars with dancing and rhythm instruments would effectively highlight the festivity of this piece.

8   By the Waters

This early American round based on the text of Psalm 137 is a most beautiful example of lamenting music. The "father of American music," William Billings, composed several rounds of this nature. It was a very important part of the Sunday ritual for the 1993 Re-Imagining Conference. This haunting melody can be used in unison or in two- or three-part canon. It is also very effective with movement and serves well as a ritual response. The range is extensive enough that an accurate key choice is important; B-flat minor is recommended.

9   Circle 'Round for Freedom ("Circle Chant")

Linda Hirschhorn's piece was used at the second and third Re-Imagining Conferences in Minnesota as well as the Thomas Moore conference on *Care of the Soul* in 1994, where a simple circle dance for groups of ten around conference tables was designed to accompany the music. The composer lives and works in California. This piece is especially intriguing in its arrangement. It can be sung as an equal-voice composition as well as SATB. By having the melody in the "middle," the harmony parts actually circle around the tune. This gives a much lighter feeling than when chords are primarily in root position. This piece is best sung unaccompanied and with a very steady pulse. A slightly pulsed rhythm accompaniment is helpful, and a moderate tempo is recommended.

10   Come and Seek the Ways of Wisdom

Ruth Duck, who teaches at Garrett-Evangelical Theological Seminary in Evanston, Illinois, is a friend and inspiration to the work of Re-Imagining. Several published volumes of her work have inspired the church for over a decade now. This particular text was used in the 1995 Re-Imagining Conference in the musical setting by Donna Kasbohm. We suggest this hymn might be done in alternating practice by singing a verse and then walking in rhythm around a table or up the aisle, improvising movement as the group desires. Including movement communicates a sense of following where the Wisdomspirit leads. The choreography does not need to be elaborate to proclaim the message.

11   Come, O Holy Spirit, Come (Wa wa wa Emimimo)

This song for invoking the Spirit has been translated into several languages and appears in most of the World Council of Churches publications. It lends itself to many uses: as a gathering processional, a response to prayers of intercession, a ritual response to blessings, or surrounding any important part of a prayer service where the Spirit needs invitation. Do not sing this too fast or it loses its ethereal quality. Women's voices may sing as notated. If men sing the melody line, then the harmony part needs to be doubled an octave lower except for the last phrase. If the group is small, consider using only the two soprano parts and improvising sounds of wind and breath during the whole-note cadences.

12 En medio de la vida (You Are the God within Life)

This sparkling, rhythmic tune is set with both the original Spanish text and an English translation. The vitality of the tune matches the description of bodily vitality in the first stanza. Accompany with guitars, piano, and percussion.

13 For Grace-filled Moments ("O Holy One")

Donna Kasbohm, a musician, liturgist, and mother of nine children, has been a faithful leader of the ritual music work for the Re-Imagining Community, having served in a musical leadership capacity at all its conferences. She is currently the music and liturgy director at St. William's Catholic Community in Fridley, Minnesota. This ritual piece was written for a blessing service for the Fifth Year Anniversary Celebration of the Theological Insights program at the College of St. Catherine in St. Paul, Minnesota, of which Donna is a graduate. Her piece might be a part of the ritual repertoire of any group of people who gather and wish to offer blessings for people, events, and especially "grace-filled" moments.

14 For the Beauty of the Earth

Although dating from the nineteenth century, this familiar text sings quite in tune with contemporary images of God's goodness and love as expressed in nature. The lovely Chinese folk song is also about nature, and many will recognize the tune from its use in Puccini's opera *Turandot*. This is a folk tune, and not to be harmonized by voices. It might be served by a pedal voice, probably on C and B-flat, and by small instruments like finger cymbals, random-pitched bells, or even tone bells.

15 From My Mother's Womb

The table conversations of the 1993 Re-Imagining Conference opened with this ritual antiphon. We "sang on," having been given our song by so many female ancestors. This simple but haunting refrain captured the hearts of the conference participants and has been heard around the country frequently since that time. Jeanne Cotter is a performer, composer, and weaver of story songs. She currently resides in California. This music serves as a blessing on the ritual work and conversations of women. It will not be difficult to find a way to contextualize this piece. It sings quite well unaccompanied, but is even more beautiful when a piano is available.

16 Gathered Here ("Gathering Chant")

Phil Porter, a California liturgical artist, has offered this round as another way of inviting the Spirit near. Singers are captivated by the strength of the phrase "gathered here in one strong body." The music supports and illustrates that phrase. Don't hesitate to accentuate it. This piece is effectively used as a call to prayer or as a gathering rite whenever Christians meet and invite the Spirit's presence.

17 GUIDE MY FEET
18 SMILE WITH ME

The whole repertoire of spirituals from the African American community cry out to God in a way unlike any other body of song. Born of oppression, the music and texts ask for liberation while extending hope. The primary metaphor of "Guide My Feet" is that of living life to the fullest. In the second text, Joan Prefontaine offers another set of stanzas that connect our prayer to God in praise for things of the earth. Jane Ramseyer Miller's harmonization intentionally places the melody line in the middle to allow for versatility. It could be used with soprano descant only, as an SAB arrangement, or as an SSA setting by singing measure five one octave higher in the lowest voice.

19 I CAME TO LIFE IN YOUR DARK WATERS ("SOPHIA")

Hilda Kuester is an ordained minister in the United Church of Christ. She wrote this text in response to a challenge to improve on Malotte's setting of "The Lord's Prayer," which is loved and sung in so many communities. Rather than altering that text to make it more inclusive, she wrote this prayer to a folk tune. This stanza-refrain form lends itself to other prayer forms as well. The refrain could be a response to intercessory prayer, prepared or spontaneous. The whole piece could be sung as a conclusion to the prayer.

20 I SING TO YOU FROM SUMMERS OF MY HEART ("TRUEST SINGING")

This rhapsodic text reflects the voice of a mystic. Jean Wiebe Janzen's poetry speaks eloquently about the possibility of faith that brings hope to flower, urged forward by the Spirit's steadfast love and presence. Feminine spirituality supports this relationship with the Godspirit. Cathy Tisel Nelson, a composer who lives and works in Rochester, Minnesota, wrote the tune. Her music captures in sound the quality of the text. The piece is at first glance a straightforward strophic hymn. Try a slight fermata on the cadence note that begins the 6/4 measure. "There flows my truest singing," which is the essence of the expression of the text writer, might be used as a springboard for reflection by a small group. From where and in what way does your "truest singing" come? Give each person a chance for personal reflection, followed by the singing of this last phrase. Hum the tune up to that point and offer the sung phrase as an affirmation of the person's reflection.

21 JOSHUA DANCED ON HOLY GROUND ("DANCING AT THE WALL")

This song honors current work for justice as well as the spiritual tradition echoed in "Joshua fit de Battle of Jericho." Jane Ramseyer Miller wrote this piece in honor of a dear and gifted friend, Greg Lichti, who finished seminary but was rejected as a pastor in his denomination because he is gay. It was sung as a surprise for Greg at a ritual marking his transition to a new vocation. Singers are encouraged to improvise additional stanzas naming those who are seekers of justice in the local community or the world at large. New stanzas may be best sung by a single voice or small group to which the whole assembly can respond at measure five. The guitar chords are designed for unison singing only. (They are not compatible with the given harmony.) When full parts are sung, accompany with rhythm instruments or piano.

22   Kyrie Eleison

This tune appears in the World Council of Churches collection from the women's gathering in 1989. The Greek liturgical text used for lament or response to intercessions is a familiar one. This music has a rhythmic weep as well as a pitch weep in the flatted third, often termed the "blue" note in jazz. This classic arch shape of the music makes it reminiscent of oral tradition, although it is in fact a carefully crafted composition by a living composer. Eight measures is long for a ritual piece, but when the emphasis is on the music and not text, this is acceptable. The Kyrie would be sung unaccompanied except for perhaps drone pitches. The Re-Imagining Community accompanied it with gestures such as "holding the gut" to express the body in grief. In order to hear the "weeping" in the rhythm, the pulse of the piece moves in a slow two, which accommodates the triplet at the cadence.

23   Like a Mother Who Has Borne Us

This hymn was inspired by Hosea's depiction of the parental aspects of God's relationship with Israel. It was first sung at a chapel service at Dickinson College, Carlisle, Pennsylvania, where Daniel Bechtel, a minister of the United Church of Christ, served as professor of religion. The flowing tune by William P. Rowan is a good companion for this text, in contrast to an even-metered tune like STUTTGART, which is the same meter.

24   Make Wide the Circle

The circle is a recurring image in the feminist movement, distinguishing it from the linear and hierarchical. This text suggests all the categories of those who need to be included more fully. Donna Kasbohm adapted this text for the 1995 Re-Imagining Conference and developed a refrain building on the closing phrase—"Love! Peace! Let us begin!" These musical elements present many possibilities for use other than simply singing the music as a stanza-refrain piece. The simple eight-measure mantra may easily be harmonized in sixths. This section could be used to accompany spoken text, as a call to prayer or gathering, or as an hummed accompaniment to the eight bars of the text.

25   Mine Is the Church ("A Dazzling Bouquet")

This tune in a swing style lifts up the inclusive church as a bouquet of flowers. Bret Hesla is a Minnesota composer who has been a part of the Community of St. Martin's in Minneapolis. He currently lives in an intentional community in Rushford. Bret's directions are "with a Cajun swing feel, or boogie woogie." This piece needs a strong guitar player and would be well served with bass, drums, and piano as well. "A Dazzling Bouquet" cries out for dancing, perhaps alternating one stanza of singing with one of dancing.

26 MOTHERING GOD, YOU GAVE ME BIRTH

Julian of Norwich was the inspiration for this trinitarian adaptation by Jean Wiebe Janzen, a Mennonite poet living in California. Jane Ramseyer Miller later wrote this lovely round in the tradition of William Billings, using four phrases of four bars with interesting hemiola. This round would be appropriate anywhere that a doxological text and response are called for: after psalms, after intercessory prayer, or as an expression of gratitude for the ways God cares for us. When teaching it, be sure that the community has a good grasp of the tune before trying it in round. Although a full four-part round, it would work in two or three parts as well. It needs to be felt in "three" (not "one") or the "across the bar" rhythms may be missed, spoiling the harmonic shape.

27 MY MOTHER'S LIFE I CELEBRATE THIS DAY

Martha Postlethwaite is the current chaplain at United Theological Seminary in Minnesota. She is an ordained clergy in the United Methodist Church. This text was a gift to her mother on Mother's Day. Her mother is a musician, and her father was a hymn text writer and a source of inspiration for his daughter. The music is a tune that appears in most hymnals with a text invoking the Spirit. This nineteenth-century hymn seemed to marry well with this contemplative reflection about mothering.

28 MYSTERY IN DARKNESS

Darkness has been lifted up in much feminist writing as a source of inspiration. Joan Prefontaine, a published poet from Northfield, Minnesota, shows her craft in several hymns in this collection. This particular piece was a part of her integrative project on the general theme of ambiguity for United Theological Seminary in the Twin Cities, where she finished her degree in 1996. Several composers have been inspired by this text. We have chosen Donna Kasbohm's setting for its simplicity and transparency.

Although this is a hymn in strophic form, it has a quasi-refrain in the second half. Kasbohm's music, which shifts to the parallel major here, helps to set that up. The lullaby-like quality of the second half might serve well as a closing for any evening service. A threefold blessing could be interspersed, or gestures of blessing for the night could be offered among the congregation as they prepare to depart.

29 NAMELESS WOMEN, FULL OF PASSION

Martha Postlethwaite wrote this hymn to accompany a sermon she was preaching at Hennepin United Methodist Church in Minneapolis, Minnesota. She lifts up in verse form the many women from the biblical text who are not named but whose stores we know well. The text sings well with BEACH SPRING, one of the familiar tunes from the Appalachian tradition. This is a more traditional hymn form in its

need to be sung in its entirety. Martha did intertwine it with her sermon, as some other preachers might consider doing.

30   O FALLING WATER

This tune is a familiar and beloved Spanish hymn. The text, inspired by the work of Rigoberta Menchu, was written in English. The refrain might be used alone in any celebration as a ritual piece, as a procession with flowers (popular in Latina cultures), for a children's service, or for any festival important to the Guatemalan calendar as celebrated locally. The stanzas might be sung by choir or another group of singers. This piece is best accompanied by guitars and/or piano.

31   O HOLY SPIRIT, ROOT OF LIFE

Hildegard who served as abbess of Bingen in the twelfth century, was a "woman for all seasons." She was a prolific composer, poet, artist, and mystic, as well as a scientist and theologian with a profound spirituality. The melody is the familiar Renaissance dance tune found in most hymnals, PUER NOBIS NASCITUR. This straightforward hymn could be a fuller expression when used with alternate verses or other music in triple meter from the period and banner poles with red ribbons inviting the Spirit's presence.

32   ON THE HORIZON ("VIRGIN GROUND")

"On the Horizon" ("Virgin Ground") is an elemental piece inviting us into reflection on and gratitude for the spirit of Mary. The complex rhythms are notated, but the spirit of the rhythm is to be free over a strict basic pulse. Gentle rhythm instruments, as well as the scat-style descant, will give life to this composition.

33   PAZ, QUEREMOS PAZ

The translation of this song from oral tradition is: "Peace, we want peace and liberty [or freedom] in this world." It should be sung in Spanish as an acclamation. Spontaneous yearnings could be voiced in between the singing. The key moves up by half steps when repeated. The harmony is simple enough for any group to learn by rote.

34   PRAISE, MY FRIEND, THIS HOLY CUP ("CUP OF BLESSING")

This text and tune were commissioned for the second Re-Imagining Conference in Minneapolis for the celebration of the cup of milk and honey. After having been dropped from Christian tradition in the third century, Re-Imagining and others are returning the cup of milk and honey to the communion ritual. This is a straightforward hymn best sung with a clear subdivision of the pulse. The deliberate tempo assures that the words can be savored. Try it with a verse of humming between the two stanzas. It might best be placed as a thanksgiving after a celebration of drinking from the cup.

35 SANNA

This delightful and exuberant hosanna in its shortened form, "Sanna," is in the tradition of South African freedom songs. Its AABB structure makes it easy to learn when taught by rote. The pulse suggests processional use; procession by all, not just a few. Palm Sunday is an obvious occasion for its use, but consider also other times in the church community when there are wonderful processions of people—confirmation classes, children returning from children's liturgy of the Word, spring pageants, etc. With this repetitive antiphon, it is not necessary for the congregation to have its noses buried in the books and miss the parade. It makes a valuable addition to the community's repertoire for more informal gatherings as well.

36 SEEKING HEALING IN OUR JOURNEY

Jane Ramseyer Miller wrote this piece for an ecumenical healing service to celebrate relief from anxiety and fear shared by a community. The text describes the way these feelings also bind the community together as it reaches out to others. This piece calls for ritual action associated with healing, as experienced in a variety of communities and styles. Miller uses the elements of water, oil, and bread in her text. Other symbols could be added or substituted according to the setting.

37 SI FUI MOTIVO DE DOLOR, OH DIOS
(IF I HAVE BEEN THE SOURCE OF PAIN, O GOD)

This prayer of lament, provided in both Spanish and English, speaks in the voice of the psalmist. It provides a new interpretation of the older hymn "If I Have Wounded Any Soul Today." Pablo Sosa, from Argentina, is a contemporary composer with international influence through his work for the World Council of Churches. The final phrase, "perdon, oh Dios," could be lifted out as a refrain in any service where reconciliation is the primary focus. Use the hymn in its entirety as a prelude to a litany prepared or spontaneous, spoken or unspoken, where people are asking for forgiveness. The haunting descending parallel fifths might serve as a choral mantra by the low voices.

38 SOPHIA AS A BREATH OF GOD

This hymn was introduced at the 1995 Re-Imagining Conference. Joan Prefontaine, the community's poet laureate, here lifts up the many images of Wisdom Sophia from Proverbs. This poem could well serve as the focus for reflection on the divine feminine as shared in the Hebrew Testament literature. Donna Kasbohm's lilting tune supports the sense of Sophia "sporting upon the wind" as it gracefully carries us through the text. The hymn needs to be sung in its entirety. For small-group use, we suggest that you sing a stanza at a time, perhaps humming the music first on a neutral syllable to enter into the playfulness of Spirit. Sing the text of one stanza and let the group reflect on the veracity of these images in their own experience. Then sing the entire text at the end as a celebration of Sophia.

39 SOPHIA, CREATOR GOD

This acclamation was written for the milk and honey ritual at the 1993 Re-Imagining Conference. Its rhythmic exuberance added much to the festivities. It was placed as a response to the text by Hilda Kuester for the blessing and celebration of women's experience at the closing ritual. The text is generic enough that milk and honey can be understood as a metaphor and the piece used in a variety of settings. Given its length, it works best when there are a number of short texts to which musical response is made. An easy equal-voice arrangement is provided with the melody in the middle. Use lots of rhythm instruments on the beat in order to keep the highly syncopated rhythm steady.

40 TAKE THE DARK STRENGTH OF OUR NIGHTS

This popular Jamaican salsa tune appears in many global song collections. We were captivated by the feminist image of "weaving a womb" in order that the community might see hope coming out of oppression. This is the Jesus message of the Christ who is overturner of systems of oppression in all its forms. This piece is another expression of the positive nature of darkness. The hopeful and playful message of this music as well as the text is to be enjoyed. The very nature of music making stimulates hope and keeps it alive. The piece is best accompanied by guitars, maracas, drums, and dancing.

41 WE ARE SHADOWS ON THE ROCK

"At Hiroshima there is a museum. Outside the museum there is a rock, and on the rock there is a shadow. The shadow is all that remains of the human being that stood there on August 6th, 1945, when the nuclear age began." This piece was written for the Shadows on the Rock Peace Camp in preparation for the fiftieth anniversary of the bombing of Hiroshima and Nagasaki. The descant is a contemporary cry of resistance to the nuclear age. This vigorous hymn really needs a four-part rendering with vocal strength and rhythmic vitality. The descant could also be used as a separate antiphon in any service where a litany of resistance might be called for. The piece would also be appropriate for Earth Day celebrations. The last phrase, "Come and heal our bleeding world," might be lifted out as an antiphon for blessing over various parts of the earth in such a service or spoken in the four directions.

Composer Jane Ramseyer Miller is a musician, performer, and choral conductor living in St. Paul, Minnesota. Because she grew up in the Mennonite Church, many of her compositions reflect the strong harmonic nature of traditional Mennonite, four-part singing. Her texts, too, are reflective of the denomination's uniqueness as a historical peace church and Miller's own commitment to issues of peace and justice.

42 WE ARE WOMEN AT THE WELL ("WOMEN AT THE WELL")

This litany celebrating women in Christian history names us all as women thirsting for the living water offered by Jesus in the familiar Gospel story. The groups of names could be expanded. For example: "We remember women in our church who have died . . ."; "We remember the women who serve faithfully in our congregation, especially . . ."; "We remember all those women important to each of us named now in our hearts." The antiphon could also be shortened by using the first four measures followed by the last four. When using the shorter antiphon, the litanies themselves need to be shorter in length.

43 WE HAVE LABORED ("WEAVING A NEW CREATION")

This ritual text as written originally for a women's worship service at the Parliament of World Religions in Chicago, Illinois, in 1993. Donna Kasbohm then developed this music for the 1996 Re-Imagining Conference. The stanza-refrain format lends itself to many performance possibilities. The music has a processional quality about it. The strong affirmation of women's work could also be used as an acclamation on any occasion where people and gifts are honored. The refrain is written as a two-part canon and works with the provided piano accompaniment in canon as well as unison. The stanzas are strong in text and tone. We suggest they be sung by a smaller group in order to achieve a layered vocal texture.

44 WHAT YOU HOLD

This composition is part of Cathy Tisel Nelson's larger collection by the same title. The Sisters of St. Francis in Rochester, Minnesota, were instrumental in supporting and encouraging that collection primarily based on texts of St. Clare and St. Francis of Assisi. Clare and Francis are the dreamers and mystics who have had people following in their footsteps through the Franciscan movement the world over. Tisel Nelson served as music director for six years with the Rochester Franciscans. This translation is the work of Regis Armstrong, OFM, Cap., based on St. Clare's second letter to Agnes of Prague. St. Clare encourages Agnes to persevere in her commitment to the radical poverty of the Poor Christ and in her commitment to her vocation in general.

The song is set as a stanza-refrain. The undulating piano accompaniment is essential to its movement and style. At the 1993 Re-Imagining Conference, this piece was used as a closing blessing over the work of the conference and the continuing commitments people had made for re-imagining work. Clare's words of centuries long ago invite us to "go forward securely and joyfully with swift pace, light step, and unswerving feet." This composition has been celebrated and sung in many contexts since 1993, a witness to its power to speak profoundly in community.

45 WHEN, LIKE THE WOMAN AT THE WELL

This hymn honors the woman at the well from John's Gospel as a model for the relationship of women to Christ. Edith Sinclair Downing began writing hymn texts in 1989 when she and her husband were Associates in Ministry with a pilot project of the Presbyterian Church (USA). Celene Welch named her tune CRAVEN, in honor of Professor Toni Craven of Texas Christian University. This hymn could appropriately accompany water blessings, baptisms, or preaching on the familiar story from John. The gentle unison melody could be accompanied by harp or guitar playing on downbeats, almost like accompanied chant.

46 WHO IS SHE?

This is one of Brian Wren's earlier hymn texts, published in 1986. In it, Wren asks the question "Who is She?" and then replies in each strophe by telling us that "She" is "God," "Love," "Life," and "Hope." Donna Kasbohm's setting supports this structure through the use of parallel minor and major for the questions and answers. Basic questions in most reflection groups are "Who is God?" and "Who are we in relation to God?" This hymn would serve well as a starter for such an event. Any occasion in the congregation which celebrates the Divine feminine could begin or end with this hymn.

47 WOMB OF LIFE, AND SOURCE OF BEING

This hymn, which mixes old and new metaphors to express faith and praise to God, is a renaming of the Trinity. The hymn borrows a phrase from Charles Wesley's familiar carol—"born to give us second birth"—which is itself a re-imagining phrase. According to Ruth Duck, trinitarian theology provides a model for the life of community. HYMN TO JOY is suggested as an alternate tune to Arnatt's more contemporary one, LADUE CHAPEL. This tune is worth learning well, but will take some repetition for the community to feel comfortable with the two-measure rhythmic pattern repeated throughout. Some of the pitch contours are unexpected. The piece calls for a gentle but accurate rhythm that is unhurried.

48 WOMEN'S VOICES, WOMEN'S WITNESS

Manley Olson is a Presbyterian layman who has been a faithful member of the Re-Imagining Council since its inception. He is a prolific writer of hymn texts. This text celebrates many women, named and unnamed, from the Bible. Olson has suggested the tune HOLY MANNA for this text. BEACH SPRING is equally effective. The old Welsh standby for this meter, HYFRYDOL, would work well also if the Appalachian tunes are not familiar.

49 YOU CALL US ("GOD, ECCLESIA")

Nancy Berneking and Sue Swanson are both council members for the Re-Imagining Community. Nancy serves as the current editor of the newsletter, and Sue has been a participant in the music of most of our conferences. The Re-Imagining Community has been offering classes in various topics relative to our work, a teaching venture called Faith Labs. This piece was conceived in a class taught by Marty Haugen where Berneking and Swanson collaborated on the composition. This hymn song names in some unusual ways how God calls us through the church, hence its refrain text: "God, Ecclesia." "Ecclesia" is the Greek word for community (church).

bring the

fEAST

1 A Prophet-Woman Broke a Jar

1 A proph-et-wom-an broke a jar, by Love's di-vine ap-point-ing.
2 A faith-ful wom-an left a tomb by Love's di-vine com-mis-sion.
3 Though wom-an-wis-dom, wom-an-truth, for cen-tu-ries were hid-den,
4 The Spir-it knows, the Spir-it calls, by Love's di-vine or-dain-ing,

With rare per-fume she filled the room, pre-sid-ing and a-noint-ing.
She saw, she heard, she preached the Word, a-ris-ing from sub-mis-sion.
un-sung, un-writ-ten, and un-heard, de-rid-ed and for-bid-den,
the friends we need, to serve and lead, their powers and gifts un-chain-ing.

A proph-et-wom-an broke a jar, the sneers of scorn de-fy-ing.
A faith-ful wom-an left a tomb, with res-ur-rec-tion gos-pel.
the Spir-it's breath, the Spir-it's fire, on free and slave de-scend-ing,
The Spir-it knows, the Spir-it calls, from wom-en, men and chil-dren,

With rare per-fume she filled the room, pre-par-ing Christ for dy-ing.
She saw, she heard, she preached the Word, a-pos-tle to a-pos-tles.
can tum-ble our di-vid-ing walls, our shame and sad-ness mend-ing.
the friends we need, to serve and lead. Re-joice, and make them wel-come!

WORDS: Brian Wren, 1991; copyright © 1993 Hope Publishing Co., Carol Stream, IL 60188.
MUSIC: PROPHET-WOMAN by Donna Kasbohm, 1996; copyright © 1997 The Pilgrim Press.

1 A Prophet-Woman Broke a Jar

1 A prophet-woman broke a jar,
   by Love's divine appointing.
   With rare perfume she filled the room,
   presiding and anointing.
   A prophet-woman broke a jar,
   the sneers of scorn defying.
   With rare perfume she filled the room,
   preparing Christ for dying.

2 A faithful woman left a tomb
   by Love's divine commission.
   She saw, she heard, she preached the Word,
   arising from submission.
   A faithful woman left a tomb,
   with resurrection gospel.
   She saw, she heard, she preached the Word,
   apostle to apostles.

3 Though woman-wisdom, woman-truth,
   for centuries were hidden,
   unsung, unwritten, and unheard,
   derided and forbidden,
   the Spirit's breath, the Spirit's fire,
   on free and slave descending,
   can tumble our dividing walls,
   our shame and sadness mending.

4 The Spirit knows, the Spirit calls,
   by Love's divine ordaining,
   the friends we need, to serve and lead,
   their powers and gifts unchaining.
   The Spirit knows, the Spirit calls,
   from women, men and children,
   the friends we need, to serve and lead.
   Rejoice, and make them welcome!

WORDS: Brian Wren, 1991; copyright © 1993 Hope Publishing Co., Carol Stream, IL 60188.
MUSIC: PROPHET-WOMAN by Donna Kasbohm, 1996; copyright © 1997 The Pilgrim Press.

2 Bless Now, O God, the Journey ("Hymn of Covenant")

then   leads be - side still wa - ters,   the   road where faith is
to - geth - er we are seek - ing   the   road where faith is
Our   cov - e - nant is writ - ten   on   roads, as faith is

Last time, end here.

found.
found.
found.

Descant for Stanza 3

Di - vine_____ lov -_____ er on the road.

Land   of prom - ise, milk and hon - ey flow._____ Wait

not,_____ meet us all a - round._____

Cov - e - nant on the road, as faith is found.

2 Bless Now, O God, the Journey
("Hymn of Covenant")

1 Bless now, O God, the journey that all your people make,
   the path through noise and silence, the way of give and take.
   The trail is found in desert, and winds the mountain round,
   then leads beside still waters, the road where faith is found.

2 Bless sojourners and pilgrims who share this winding way,
   whose hope burns through the terrors, whose love sustains the day.
   We yearn for holy freedom while often we are bound;
   together we are seeking the road where faith is found.

3 Divine eternal lover, you meet us on the road.
   We wait for land of promise where milk and honey flow,
   but waiting not for places, you meet us all around.
   Our covenant is written on roads, as faith is found.

WORDS: Sylvia Dunstan; copyright © 1991 G.I.A. Publications, Inc.
MUSIC: PASCAL JOURNEY by Madelin Sue Martin; copyright © 1997 The Pilgrim Press.

3 Bless Sophia

Bless So - phi - a, dream the vi - sion,

share the wis - dom dwell - ing deep with - in.

(percussion ad lib.)

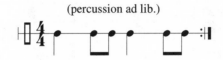

WORDS: David Haas; copyright © 1997 The Pilgrim Press.
MUSIC: "E Na Lima Hana," Hawaiian chant, adapt.; copyright © 1997 G.I.A. Publications, Inc.

3 Bless Sophia

Bless Sophia,
dream the vision,
share the wisdom
dwelling deep within.

WORDS: David Haas; copyright © 1997 The Pilgrim Press.
MUSIC: "E Na Lima Hana," Hawaiian chant, adapt.; copyright © 1997 G.I.A. Publications, Inc.

4 Blessed Are the Persecuted (Sean benditos los que sufren)

1 Bless-ed are the per-se-cut-ed, for Je-sus Christ is liv-ing with-in them.
2 Bless-ed are they who are hun-gry in Spir-it, for our God lives with-in them.
1 Sean ben-di-tos los que su-fren ha-cien-do lo que Dios les ha man-da-do.
2 Sean ben-di-tos los que tie-nen lim-pio el co-ra-zón, ve-rán a Dios.

Estribillo (Refrain)

Great will be their re-ward, they shall be giv'n a crown,
He - re - da - rán el Rei - no del Se - ñor Je - sús

Last time, end here.

when our God comes from heav'n to meet them.
cuan - do ven - gan a rei - nar por siem - pre.

3 Sean ben-di-tos los hu-mil-des
re-ci-bi-rán de Dios to-da la tie-rra.

4 Sean ben-di-tos los se-dien-tos
vi-ve en e-llos nues-tro Se-ñor.

3 Blessed are the pure in heart,
for Jesus Christ is living within them.

4 Blessed are they who are thirsty in Spirit,
for our God lives within them.

1 Balaacoolwe bapenzegwa
Nkaambo kaJesu mumyoyo yabo.

Refrain
Baya kutambula musyini wabuumi
Akuboola iMwami Jesu.

2 Balaacoolwe bafwa nzala
Yakumuuya mumyoyo yabo.

3 Balaacoolwe basalala
Nkaambo ka-Jesu mumyoyo yabo.

4 Balaacoolwe bafwa nyota
Yakumuuya mumyoyo yabo.

WORDS: Based on Matthew 5; adapt. Esther C. Bergen; Spanish trans. Betty Puricelli;
copyright © 1990 Mennonite World Conference, Strasbourg, France;
Tonga text reprinted by permission of the Brethren in Christ Church, Zambia.
MUSIC: Tonga melody (Zambia).

4 Blessed Are the Persecuted
(Sean benditos los que sufren)

1 Blessed are the persecuted,
   for Jesus Christ is living within them.
   Refrain: Great will be their reward,
                   they shall be giv'n a crown,
                   when our God comes from heav'n to meet them.

2 Blessed are they who are hungry in Spirit,
   for our God lives within them.
   Refrain

3 Blessed are the pure in heart,
   for Jesus Christ is living within them.
   Refrain

4 Blessed are they who are thirsty in Spirit,
   for our God lives within them.
   Refrain

1 Sean benditos los que sufren
   haciendo lo que Dios les ha mandado.
   Estribillo: Heredarán el Reino del Señor Jesús
                      cuando vengan a reinar por siempre.

2 Sean benditos los que tienen
   limpio el corazón, verán a Dios.
   Estribillo

3 Sean benditos los humildes
   recibirán de Dios toda la tierra.
   Estribillo

4 Sean benditos los sedientos
   vive en ellos nuestro Señor.
   Estribillo

WORDS: Based on Matthew 5; adapt. Esther C. Bergen; Spanish trans. Betty Puricelli;
   copyright © 1990 Mennonite World Conference, Strasbourg, France.
MUSIC: Tonga melody (Zambia)

5 Braided Rugs ("Braided Lives")

Flute descant

Unison C   Em   Am   Dm

Braid- ed rugs, braid- ed hopes, braid- ed lives, braid- ed souls.

Em   Am   Em7   F   Am7   Em

Sewn to - geth - er sing- ing, joined to - geth - er weep - ing. Heal our hearts.

F   G   C/G   G7   C   Am

Hear our prayer.

WORDS AND MUSIC: Jane Ramseyer Miller, 1996; copyright © 1997 The Pilgrim Press.

5 Braided Rugs ("Braided Lives")

Braided rugs,	Sewn together singing,
braided hopes,	joined together weeping.
braided lives,	Heal our hearts.
braided souls.	Hear our prayer.

WORDS AND MUSIC: Jane Ramseyer Miller, 1996; copyright © 1997 The Pilgrim Press.

6 Bring Many Names

1 Bring man-y names, beau-ti-ful and good, cel-e-brate, in par-a-ble and sto-ry, ho-li-ness in glo-ry, liv-ing, lov-ing God. Hail and Ho-san-na! bring man-y names!

2 Strong moth-er God, work-ing night and day, plan-ning all the won-ders of cre-a-tion, set-ting each e-qua-tion, gen-i-us at play: Hail and Ho-san-na, strong moth-er God!

3 Warm fa-ther God, hug-ging ev-'ry child, feel-ing all the strains of hu-man liv-ing, car-ing and for-giv-ing, till we're rec-on-ciled: Hail and Ho-san-na, warm fath-er God!

4 Old, ach-ing God, grey with end-less care, calm-ly pierc-ing e-vil's new dis-guis-es, glad of good sur-pris-es, wis-er than de-spair: Hail and Ho-san-na, old, ach-ing God!

5 Young, grow-ing God, ea-ger, on the move, say-ing no to false-hood and un-kind-ness, cry-ing out for jus-tice, giv-ing all you have: Hail and Ho-san-na, young, grow-ing God!

6 Great, liv-ing God, nev-er ful-ly known, joy-ful dark-ness far be-yond our see-ing, clos-er yet than breath-ing, ev-er-last-ing home: Hail and Ho-san-na, great, liv-ing God!

WORDS: Brian Wren, 1989; copyright © 1989, 1994 Hope Publishing Co., Carol Stream, IL 60188.
MUSIC: RIDGEVIEW by Donna B. Kasbohm; copyright © 1993 World Library Publications, a division of J.S. Paluch Company, Inc., Schiller Park, IL. All rights reserved. Used by permission.

6 Bring Many Names

1 Bring many names, beautiful and good,
celebrate, in parable and story,
holiness in glory, living, loving God.
Hail and Hosanna! bring many names!

2 Strong mother God, working night and day,
planning all the wonders of creation,
setting each equation, genius at play:
Hail and Hosanna, strong mother God!

3 Warm father God, hugging ev'ry child,
feeling all the strains of human living,
caring and forgiving till we're reconciled:
Hail and Hosanna, warm father God!

4 Old, aching God, grey with endless care,
calmly piercing evil's new disguises,
glad of good surprises, wiser than despair:
Hail and Hosanna, old, aching God!

5 Young, growing God, eager, on the move,
saying no to falsehood and unkindness,
crying out for justice, giving all you have:
Hail and Hosanna, young, growing God!

6 Great, living God, never fully known,
joyful darkness far beyond our seeing,
closer yet than breathing, everlasting home:
Hail and Hosanna, great, living God!

WORDS: Brian Wren, 1989; copyright © 1989, 1994 Hope Publishing Co., Carol Stream, IL 60188.
MUSIC: RIDGEVIEW by Donna B. Kasbohm; copyright © 1993 World Library Publications, a division
of J.S. Paluch Company, Inc., Schiller Park, IL. All rights reserved. Used by permission.

7 Bring the Feast to Ev'ry Hillside

1 Bring the feast to ev-'ry hill-side, where the hun-gry peo-ple wait.
2 Bring the feast to ev-'ry hide-out where the poor and thirst-y dwell,
3 Who will love de-sert-ed spac-es? Who will share a strang-er's cup?
4 Danc-ing at in-clu-sive ta-bles, gay and straight to-geth-er sing.

Loaves and fish-es mul-ti-ply-ing: com-mon mir-a-cles cre-ate!
cries of pain and des-per-a-tion, card-board shel-ters, pris-on cells.
Who will bless those no one bless-es? Who will speak and dare stand up?
Join with us to strength-en, nur-ture, let our jus-tice voic-es ring!

While some choose to keep their ta-ble where a wealth-y few can dine,
Where there is no grass to rest on, where the earth's been paved and torn,
O Cre-a-tor, Life Sus-tain-er, spark of hope in young and old,
Bread that knows no gen-dered lan-guage, grapes of sol-i-dar-i-ty;

Let us praise a wid-er ven-ture: mov-ing ban-quets, bread and wine.
let us spread com-mu-nal ta-bles till in-jus-tice is out-worn.
help us spread and move the ta-ble where we of-ten fear to go.
Sis-ters, broth-ers, join the Love Feast, dance to shape com-mu-ni-ty!

WORDS: Joan Prefontaine, 1996; copyright © 1997 The Pilgrim Press.
MUSIC: FEAST by Jane Ramseyer Miller; copyright © 1997 The Pilgrim Press.

7 Bring the Feast to Ev'ry Hillside

1 Bring the feast to ev'ry hillside
   where the hungry people wait.
   Loaves and fishes multiplying:
   common miracles create!
   While some choose to keep their table
   where a wealthy few can dine,
   let us praise a wider venture:
   moving banquets, bread and wine.

2 Bring the feast to ev'ry hideout
   where the poor and thirsty dwell,
   cries of pain and desperation,
   cardboard shelters, prison cells.
   Where there is no grass to rest on,
   where the earth's been paved and torn,
   let us spread communal tables
   till injustice is outworn.

3 Who will love deserted spaces?
   Who will share a stranger's cup?
   Who will bless those no one blesses?
   Who will speak and dare stand up?
   O Creator, Life Sustainer,
   spark of hope in young and old,
   help us spread and move the table
   where we often fear to go.

4 Dancing at inclusive tables,
   gay and straight together sing.
   Join with us to strengthen, nurture,
   let our justice-voices ring!
   Bread that knows no gendered language,
   grapes of solidarity;
   Sisters, brothers, join the Love Feast,
   dance to shape community.

WORDS: Joan Prefontaine, 1996; copyright © 1997 The Pilgrim Press.
MUSIC: FEAST by Jane Ramseyer Miller; copyright © 1997 The Pilgrim Press.

8 By the Waters

By the   wa - ters,   by the   wa - ters,   by the   wa - ters,   Ba - by - lon.

We   sat   down   and   wept,   and   wept   for   thee,   Zi - on.

We   re - mem - ber,   we   re - mem - ber,   we   re - mem - ber   thee,   Zi - on.

WORDS: Based on Psalm 137.
MUSIC: William Billings.

8 By the Waters

By the waters, by the waters, by the waters, Babylon.
We sat down and wept, and wept for thee, Zion.
We remember, we remember, we remember thee, Zion.

WORDS: Based on Psalm 137.
MUSIC: William Billings.

9 Circle 'Round for Freedom ("Circle Chant")

Circle 'round for freedom,   Circle for the planet,
circle 'round for peace,   circle for each soul,
for all of us imprisoned,   for the children of our children,
circle for release.   keep the circle whole.

WORDS AND MUSIC: As recorded in "Roots and Wings" by Linda Hirschhorn;
   copyright © 1985 Linda Hirschhorn.

9 Circle 'Round for Freedom

Melody

Cir-cle 'round for free-dom, cir-cle 'round for peace, for all of us im-

Cir-cle 'round for free-dom, cir-cle 'round for peace, for all of us im-

pris-oned, cir-cle for re-lease. Cir-cle for the plan-et, cir-cle for each

pris-oned, cir-cle for re-lease. Cir-cle for the plan-et, cir-cle for each

soul, for the chil-dren of our chil-dren, keep the cir - cle whole.

soul, for the chil-dren of our chil-dren, keep the cir - cle whole.

WORDS AND MUSIC: As recorded in "Roots and Wings" by Linda Hirschhorn;
copyright © 1985 Linda Hirschhorn.

10 Come and Seek the Ways of Wisdom

1 Come and seek the ways of Wis-dom, she who danced when
2 Lis - ten to the voice of Wis-dom, cry - ing in the
3 Sis - ter Wis-dom, come, as-sist us; nur - ture all who

earth was new. Fol - low close - ly what she teach - es,
mar - ket - place. Hear the Word made flesh a - mong us,
seek re - birth. Spir - it - guide and close com - pan - ion,

for her words are right and true. Wis - dom clears the
full of glo - ry, truth, and grace. When the word takes
bring to light our sa - cred worth. Free us to be -

WORDS: Ruth C. Duck, 1993; copyright © 1996 The Pilgrim Press.
MUSIC: MADELEINE by Donna Kasbohm, 1995; copyright © 1997 The Pilgrim Press.

path   to   jus - tice,   show - ing   us   what   love   must do.
root   and rip - ens,   peace   and righ - teous - ness em - brace.
come   your peo - ple,   ho - ly friends of   God   and earth.

10 Come and Seek the Ways of Wisdom

1 Come and seek the ways of Wisdom,
   she who danced when earth was new.
   Follow closely what she teaches,
   for her words are right and true.
   Wisdom clears the path to justice,
   showing us what love must do.

2 Listen to the voice of Wisdom,
   crying in the marketplace.
   Hear the Word made flesh among us,
   full of glory, truth, and grace.
   When the word takes root and ripens,
   peace and righteousness embrace.

3 Sister Wisdom, come, assist us;
   nurture all who seek rebirth.
   Spirit-guide and close companion,
   bring to light our sacred worth.
   Free us to become your people,
   holy friends of God and earth.

WORDS: Ruth Duck, 1993; copyright © 1997 The Pilgrim Press.
MUSIC: MADELIN by Donna Kasbohm, 1995; copyright © 1997 The Pilgrim Press.

11 Come, O Holy Spirit, Come ("Wa wa wa Emimimo")

Congregation

Come, O Ho - ly Spir - it,   come.
Wa   wa   wa   E - mi - mi - mo.

Leader

Come, al - might - y Spir - it,
Wa   wa   wa   A - lag - ba -

Ho - ly Spir - it, come.
E - mi - o - lo - ye.

come.
ra.

Come,   come,   come.
Wa   wa - o,   wa - o.

Al - might - y Spir - it, come.
A - lag - ba - ra - me - ta.

O Spir - it, come.
E - mi - mi - mo.

WORDS: Nigerian traditional, trans. I-to Loh; copyright © 1986 I-to Loh, Tainan, Taiwan,
    and WCC Geneva, Switzerland.
MUSIC: Tune copyright © The Church of the Lord (Aladura) Worldwide, Sagamu,
    Remo-Ogun State, Nigeria; arr. I-to Loh, copyright © 1986 I-to Loh and WCC.

11 Come, O Holy Spirit, Come
(Wa wa wa Emimimo)

Come, O Holy Spirit, come.
(Holy Spirit, come.)
Come, almighty Spirit, come.
(Almighty Spirit, come.)
Come, come, come.
(O Spirit, come.)

Wa wa wa Emimimo.
(Emioloye.)
Wa wa wa Alagbara.
(Alagbarameta.)
Wa wao wao.
(Emimimo.)

WORDS: Nigerian traditional, trans. I-to Loh; copyright © 1986 I-to Loh, Tainan, Taiwan,
    and WCC Geneva, Switzerland.
MUSIC: Tune copyright © The Church of the Lord (Aladura) Worldwide, Sagamu,
    Remo-Ogun State, Nigeria; arr. I-to Loh, copyright © 1986 I-to Loh and WCC.

12 En medio de la vida ("You are the God within Life")

1 En me - dio de la vi - da es - tás pre - sen - te oh Dios,
2 Tú es - tás en el tra - ba - jo del cam - po o la ciu - dad
1 You are the God with - in life, pres - ent wher - e'er we live,
2 At work we feel your pres - ence, in coun - try, cit - y, town.

mas cer - ca que mi a - lien - to, sus - ten - to de mi ser.
Y es him - no de la vi - da el dia - rio tra - ji - nar.
clos - er than all our sigh - ing, sus - tain - ing pow'r you give.
The theme of dai - ly liv - ing has mu - sic all its own –

Tú im - pul - sas en mis ve - nas mi san - gre al pal - pi - tar
El gol - pe del mar - ti - llo, la te - cla al es - cri - bir
In - side our ver - y bod - ies, you pump the blood of life;
in field, ca - reer, and busi - ness, the hum of - fice days –

y el rit - mo de la vi - da vas dan - do al co - ra - zón.
en - to - nan su a - la - ban - za al Dios de la crea - ción.
rhy - thm in ev - 'ry heart - beat drums out the pulse of life.
As - cends to our Cre - a - tor, as sym - pho - nies of praise.

WORDS: Spanish text, Mortimer Arias; English trans. st. 1, 3, George Lockwood;
copyright © 1979 Mortimer Arias, Uruguay; st. 2 by Esther C. Bergen;
copyright © 1990 Mennonite World Conference, Strasbourg, France.
MUSIC: Antonio Auza, Bolivia; copyright © 1979 Antonio Auza inheritors.

Oh Dios de cie-lo y tie-rra, te sir-vo des-de a-quí:
O God of earth and heav-en, we serve you where we are.

te a-mo en mis her-ma-nos, te a-do-ro en la cre-a-ción.
We love you in all peo-ple, we praise you in your world!

3   Tú es-tás en la a-le-grí-a y es-tás en el do-lor,
com-par-tes con tu pue-blo, la lu-cha por el bien.
En Cris-to tú has ve-ni-do la vi-da a re-di-mir
y en pren-da de tu Rei-no el mun-do a con-ver-tir.

3   We feel you in our suff'ring, and in our happiness,
fighting for human welfare, sharing with ev'ryone.
In Christ, the Incarnation, you have redeemed our lives,
pledging to us your kindom, you came, the world to change.

12 En medio de la vida (You Are the God within Life)

1 En medio de la vida estás presente oh Dios,
mas cerca que mi aliento, sustento de mi ser.
Tú impulsas en mis venas mi sangre al palpitar
y el ritmo de la vida vas dando al corazón.
Estribillo: Oh Dios de cielo y tierra, te sirvo desde aquí:
te amo en mis hermanos, te adoro en la creación.

2 Tú estás en el trabajo del campo o la ciudad
Y es himno de la vida el diario trajinar.
El golpe del martillo, la tecla al escribir
entonan su alabanza al Dios de la creación.
Estribillo

3 Tú estás en la alegría y estás en el dolor,
compartes con tu pueblo, la lucha por el bien.
En Cristo tú has venido la vida a redimir
y en prenda de tu Reino el mundo a convertir.
Estribillo

1 You are the God within life, present where'er we live,
closer than all our sighing, sustaining pow'r you give.
Inside our very bodies, you pump the blood of life;
rhythm in ev'ry heartbeat drums out the pulse of life.
Refrain: O God of earth and heaven, we serve you where we are.
We love you in all people, we praise you in your world!

2 At work we feel your presence, in country, city, town.
The theme of daily living has music all its own—
in field, career, and business, the hum of office days—
Ascends to our Creator, as symphonies of praise.
Refrain

3 We feel you in our suff'ring, and in our happiness,
fighting for human welfare, sharing with ev'ryone.
In Christ, the Incarnation, you have redeemed our lives,
pledging to us your kindom, you came, the world to change.
Refrain

WORDS: Spanish text, Mortimer Arias; English trans. st. 1, 3, George Lockwood; copyright © 1979
Mortimer Arias, Uruguay; st. 2 by Esther C. Bergen; copyright © 1990 by Mennonite World
Conference, Strasbourg, France.
MUSIC: Antonio Auza, Bolivia; copyright © 1979 Antonio Auza inheritors.

13 For Grace-Filled Moments

For grace - filled mo - ments, thanks and praise, O

Ho - ly One of Bless - ing! We hun - ger for whole - ness,

cry for jus - tice, bear - ing life in - to our world.

WORDS AND MUSIC: Donna Kasbohm, 1992; copyright © 1997 The Pilgrim Press.

13 For Grace-Filled Moments

For grace-filled moments, thanks and praise,
O Holy One of Blessing!
We hunger for wholeness, cry for justice,
bearing life into our world.

WORDS AND MUSIC: Donna Kasbohm, 1992; copyright © 1997 The Pilgrim Press.

14 For the Beauty of the Earth

Worshipfully ♩= 80

1 For the beau-ty of the earth, for the glo-ry of the skies,
2 For the won-der of each hour of the day and of the night,
3 For the joy of ear and eye, for the heart and mind's de-light,
4 For the joy of hu-man love, broth-er, sis-ter, par-ent, child,

For the love which from our birth o-ver and a-round us lies:
Hill and vale, and tree and flow'r, sun and moon, and stars of light:
For the mys-tic har-mo-ny link-ing sense to sound and sight:
Friends on earth, and friends a-bove; for all gen-tle thoughts and mild:

Refrain

Source of all, to you we raise this our hymn of

praise, this our hymn of grate-ful praise.

WORDS: Folliott S. Pierpoint, 1864; alt.
MUSIC: Chinese folk song, "Mo-li-hua"; adapt. I-to Loh, 1980; copyright © 1983 I-to Loh.

14 For the Beauty of the Earth

1   For the beauty of the earth,
    for the glory of the skies,
    For the love which from our birth
    over and around us lies:
    Refrain: Source of all, to you we raise
                      this our hymn of praise,
                      this our hymn of grateful praise.

2   For the wonder of each hour
    of the day and of the night,
    Hill and vale, and tree and flow'r,
    sun and moon, and stars of light:
    Refrain

3   For the joy of ear and eye,
    for the heart and mind's delight,
    For the mystic harmony
    linking sense to sound and sight:
    Refrain

4   For the joy of human love,
    brother, sister, parent, child,
    Friends on earth, and friends above;
    for all gentle thoughts and mild:
    Refrain

WORDS: Folliott S. Pierpoint, 1864; alt.
MUSIC: Chinese folk song, "Mo-li-hua"; adapt. I-to Loh, 1980; copyright © 1983 I-to Loh.

15 From My Mother's Womb

From my moth - er's womb and grand - moth - er's tongue,

I have heard my name, been giv - en my song.

With their blood and their beau - ty I have grown strong.

With the fire of love and rage I will sing on!

15 From My Mother's Womb

From my mother's womb and grandmother's tongue,
I have heard my name, been given my song.
With their blood and their beauty I have grown strong.
With the fire of love and rage I will sing on!

WORDS AND MUSIC: Jeanne Cotter; copyright © 1998 Jeanne Cotter/Mythic Rain.

16 Gathered Here ("Gathering Chant")

Gath - ered here in the mys - t'ry of this hour, gath - ered here in one strong bod - y,

gath - ered here in the strug - gle and the pow'r, Spir - it draw near.

WORDS AND MUSIC: Phil Porter, 1992; copyright © 1992 Phil Porter, Oakland, CA.

16 Gathered Here ("Gathering Chant")

Gathered here in the myst'ry of this hour,
Gathered here in one strong body,
Gathered here in the struggle and the pow'r,
Spirit draw near.

WORDS AND MUSIC: Phil Porter, 1990; copyright © 1992 Phil Porter, Oakland, CA.

17 Guide My Feet

2 Hold my hand . . .
3 Stand by me . . .
4 I'm your child . . .
5 Search my heart . . .

WORDS AND MUSIC: African American spiritual; arr. Jane Ramseyer Miller, 1997;
copyright © 1997 The Pilgrim Press.

18 Smile with Me

WORDS: Joan Prefontaine, 1996; copyright © 1997 The Pilgrim Press.
MUSIC: African American spiritual; arr. Jane Ramseyer Miller, 1997; copyright © 1997 The Pilgrim Press.

17 Guide My Feet

1 Guide my feet while I run this race.
Guide my feet while I run this race.
Guide my feet while I run this race,
For I don't want to run this race in vain,

2 Hold my hand . . .
For I don't want to run this race in vain.

3 Stand by me . . .
For I don't want to run this race in vain.

4 I'm your child . . .
For I don't want to run this race in vain.

5 Search my heart . . .
For I don't want to run this race in vain.

WORDS AND MUSIC: African American spiritual; arr. Jane Ramseyer Miller, 1997;
copyright © 1997 The Pilgrim Press.

18 Smile with Me

1 Smile with me while I sing your praise.
Smile with me while I sing your praise.
Smile with me while I sing your praise,
For you have made the sun to shine on earth!

2 Weep with me . . .
For you have made the stars to shine on earth!

3 Lift my heart . . .
For you have made the moon to shine on earth!

4 Comfort me . . .
For you have made the light to shine on earth!

WORDS: Joan Prefontaine, 1996; copyright © 1997 The Pilgrim Press.
MUSIC: African American spiritual; arr. Jane Ramseyer Miller, 1997; copyright © 1997
The Pilgrim Press.

19 I Came to Life in Your Dark Waters ("Sophia")

1 I came to life in your dark wa-
2 You soar a - bove me like a great ea-
3 You are cre - a - tion, you are still wa-

ters, made for the earth, con - ceived in your sea.
gle. I find my com - fort be - neath your wings.
ters, you are the pas - ture, you are the sea.

And when I'm bro - ken, lost in some des-
And when I go through the dark - est val-
You are So - phi - a, my source, my wis-

WORDS: Hilda Kuester; copyright © 1997 The Pilgrim Press.
MUSIC: CARRICKFERGUS, Irish folk melody; arr. Nancy Read Hendricks;
copyright © 1997 The Pilgrim Press.

bors,   I cry, "My Moth - er,   come shel - ter me."

19 I Came to Life in Your Dark Waters ("Sophia")

1 I came to life in your dark waters,
made for the earth, conceived in your sea.
And when I'm broken, lost in some desert,
you'll spill your life's blood to rescue me.

Refrain: Some call you "Lord," some call you "Father,"
some say "the Godhead," some "Trinity."
But when I'm aching from life's hard labors,
I cry, "My Mother, come shelter me."

2 You soar above me like a great eagle.
I find my comfort beneath your wings.
And when I go through the darkest valleys,
you are the one friend always with me.
Refrain

3 You are creation, you are still waters,
you are the pasture, you are the sea.
You are Sophia, my source, my wisdom,
you are the true light guiding me.
Refrain

Words: Hilda Kuester; copyright © 1997 The Pilgrim Press.
Music: CARRICKFERGUS, Irish folk melody; arr. Nancy Read Hendricks;
   copyright © 1997 The Pilgrim Press.

20 I Sing to You from Summers of My Heart ("Truest Singing")

1 I sing to you from sum-mers of my heart, my
(2 I) sing when full-ness bur-nish-es my day, the
(3 But) when in si-lence noth-ing ris-es up, my

voice a field of surge and green-ing, my roots es-tab-lished in the long lit
mel-low spic-es of com-ple-tion. The har-vest of my life in you which
soul is still and I am fro-zen; when i-ron days re-fuse to split and

hours, your pres-ence in the throb-bing. 2 I
yields a juice of joy and feast-ing. 3 But
thaw the clutch of ice to flow-ing— 4 Then

WORDS: Jean Wiebe Janzen, 1993; copyright © 1993 Jean Wiebe Janzen.
MUSIC: Cathy Tisel Nelson, 1996; copyright © 1996 Cathy Tisel Nelson, Rochester, MN.

(4) give me faith that warmth will swell the bud, so like a leaf my song can o-pen. For from the urg-ings of your stead-fast love, there flows my tru-est sing - ing.

20 I Sing to You from Summers of My Heart ("Truest Singing")

1 I sing to you from summers of my heart,
my voice a field of surge and greening,
my roots established in the long-lit hours,
your presence in the throbbing.

2 I sing when fullness burnishes my day,
the mellow spices of completion.
The harvest of my life in you which yields
a juice of joy and feasting.

3 But when in silence nothing rises up,
my soul is still and I am frozen;
when iron days refuse to split and thaw
the clutch of ice to flowing—

4 Then give me faith that warmth will swell the bud,
so like a leaf my song can open.
For from the urgings of your steadfast love,
there flows my truest singing.

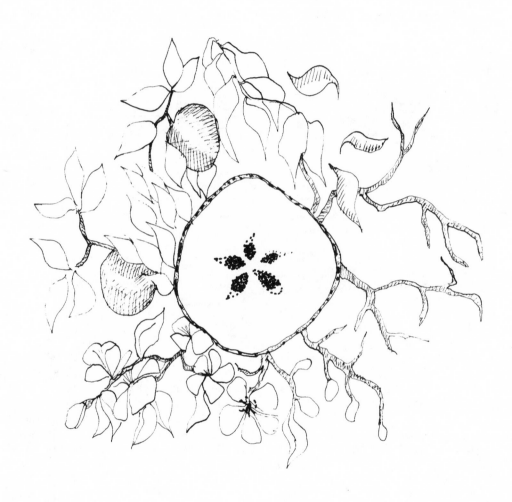

21 Joshua Danced on Holy Ground ("Dancing at the Wall")

Lively; with vigor ♩ = **126**

1 Josh - ua danced on ho - ly ground.
2 Mir - iam danced, tam - bou - rine in hand.
3 Ro - sa Parks danced by sit - ting down.
4 Har - vey Milk danced at Cit - y Hall,
5 Greg Lich - ti danced for his moth - er faith.

The Jeri - cho walls came a - tum - blin' down.
She led her peo - ple to the free - dom land.
She start - ed a boy - cott in her town.
For gay and straight, for one and all.
His gift - ed steps blew them all a - way.

Go on, Josh - ua! Dance till dawn 'cause the walls of fear are tum - bl - in' down.
Go on, Mir - iam! Dance till dawn 'cause the walls of fear are tum - bl - in' down.
Go on, Ro - sa! Dance till dawn 'cause the walls of fear are tum - bl - in' down.
Go on, Har - vey! Dance till dawn 'cause the walls of fear are tum - bl - in' down.
Go on, Greg! Dance till dawn 'cause the walls of fear are tum - bl - in' down.

Singers are encouraged to make up and sing out additional verses for the first four measures.
These can be sung by an individual with other singers responding with "Go on . . .!"
Guitar chords are intended for unison singing only. Guitarists may want to capo 3 and play in Em.

WORDS AND MUSIC: Jane Ramseyer Miller, 1995; copyright © 1997 The Pilgrim Press.

6   Sarah dared to laugh at God,
      But nine months later she delivered a child.
      Refrain

7   Esther danced before the king.
      To save her people she risked everything.
      Refrain

21 Joshua Danced on Holy Ground ("Dancing at the Wall")

1 Joshua danced on holy ground.
The Jericho walls came a-tumblin' down.
Go on, Joshua! Dance till dawn
'cause the walls of fear are tumblin' down.
Refrain: Come, dance, join our song.
                    The work of justice has begun.
                    Lift your voice, dance one and all.
                    Justice will prevail and the walls will fall.

2 Miriam danced, tambourine in hand.
She led her people to the freedom land.
Go on, Miriam! Dance till dawn
'cause the walls of fear are tumblin' down.
Refrain

3 Rosa Parks danced by sitting down.
She started a boycott in her town.
Go on, Rosa! Dance till dawn
'cause the walls of fear are tumblin' down.
Refrain

4 Harvey Milk danced at City Hall,
for gay and straight, for one and all.
Go on, Harvey! Dance till dawn
'cause the walls of fear are tumblin' down.
Refrain

5 Greg Lichti danced for his mother faith.
His gifted steps blew them all away.
Go on, Greg! Dance till dawn
'cause the walls of fear are tumblin' down.
Refrain

6 Sarah dared to laugh at God,
but nine months later she delivered a child.
Go on, Sarah! Dance till dawn
'cause the walls of fear are tumblin' down.
Refrain

7 Esther danced before the king.
To save her people she risked everything.
Go on, Esther! Dance till dawn
'cause the walls of fear are tumblin' down.
Refrain

WORDS AND MUSIC: Jane Ramseyer Miller, 1995; copyright © 1997 The Pilgrim Press.

22 Kyrie Eleison

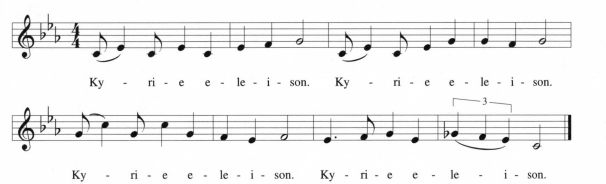

Ky - ri - e e - le - i - son. Ky - ri - e e - le - i - son.

Ky - ri - e e - le - i - son. Ky - ri - e e - le - i - son.

WORDS: Traditional.
MUSIC: Copyright © Dinah Reindorf, P.O. Box 13060, Accra, Ghana.

22 Kyrie Eleison

Kyrie eleison.
Kyrie eleison.
Kyrie eleison.
Kyrie eleison.

WORDS: Traditional.
MUSIC: Copyright © Dinah Reindorf, P.O. Box 13060, Accra, Ghana.

23 Like a Mother Who Has Borne Us

Unison

1 Like a moth - er who has borne us, held us close in her de - light, Fed us free - ly from her bod - y, God has called us in - to life._____

2 Like a fa - ther who has taught us, grasped our hand and been our guide, Lift - ed us and healed our sor - rows, God has walked with us in life._____

3 Though as chil - dren we have wan - dered, placed our trust in pow'r and might, Left be - hind our broth - ers, sis - ters, God still calls us in - to life._____

4 When we of - fer food and com - fort, grasp our neigh - bor's hand in love, Tread the path of peace and jus - tice, God still walks with us in life._____

WORDS: Daniel Bechtel, 1986; copyright © 1986 Daniel Bechtel.
MUSIC: AUSTIN by William P. Rowan, 1992; copyright © 1993 Selah Publishing Co., Inc.

23 Like a Mother Who Has Borne Us

1 Like a mother who has borne us,
   held us close in her delight,
   Fed us freely from her body,
   God has called us into life.

2 Like a father who has taught us,
   grasped our hand and been our guide,
   Lifted us and healed our sorrows,
   God has walked with us in life.

3 Though as children we have wandered,
   placed our trust in pow'r and might,
   Left behind our brothers, sisters,
   God still calls us into life.

4 When we offer food and comfort,
   grasp our neighbor's hand in love,
   Tread the path of peace and justice,
   God still walks with us in life.

WORDS: Daniel Bechtel, 1986; copyright © 1986 Daniel Bechtel.
MUSIC: AUSTIN by William P. Rowan, 1992; copyright © 1993 Selah Publishing Co., Inc.

24 Make Wide the Circle

1 Make wide the cir - cle, let all our sis - ters in! In ev - er - wide - ning cir - cles let love and peace be - gin!
2 Make wide the cir - cle and let the chil - dren in! In ev - er - wide - ning cir - cles let love and peace be - gin!
3 Make wide the cir - cle and let the old folks in! In ev - er - wide - ning cir - cles let love and peace be - gin!
4 Make wide the cir - cle and let the neigh - bors in! In ev - er - wide - ning cir - cles let love and peace be - gin!
5 Make wide the cir - cle and let the cit - y in! In ev - er - wide - ning cir - cles let love and peace be - gin!

Love! Peace! Let us be-gin. Love! Peace! Let us be-gin. Oh,

Love! Peace! Let us be-gin. Love! Peace! Let us be-gin.

6   Make wide the circle and let the nation in! . . .

7   Make wide the circle and let the cultures in! . . .

8   Make wide the circle and let the races in! . . .

9   Make wide the circle and let the whold world in! . . .

24 Make Wide the Circle

1 Make wide the circle,
   let all our sisters in!
   In ever-widening circles
   let love and peace begin!
   Refrain: Love! Peace! Let us begin.
                   Love! Peace! Let us begin. Oh,
                   Love! Peace! Let us begin.
                   Love! Peace! Let us begin.

2 Make wide the circle
   and let the children in! . . . *Refrain*

3 Make wide the circle
   and let the old folks in! . . . *Refrain*

4 Make wide the circle
   and let the neighbors in! . . . *Refrain*

5 Make wide the circle
   and let the city in! . . . *Refrain*

6 Make wide the circle
   and let the nation in! . . . *Refrain*

7 Make wide the circle
   and let all cultures in! . . . *Refrain*

8 Make wide the circle
   and let all races in! . . . *Refrain*

9 Make wide the circle
   and let the whole world in! . . . *Refrain*

WORDS: Rae E. Whitney, 1993; st. 1 adapt.; copyright © 1994 Selah Publishing Co., Inc.
MUSIC: Donna Kasbohm, 1995; copyright © 1997 The Pilgrim Press.

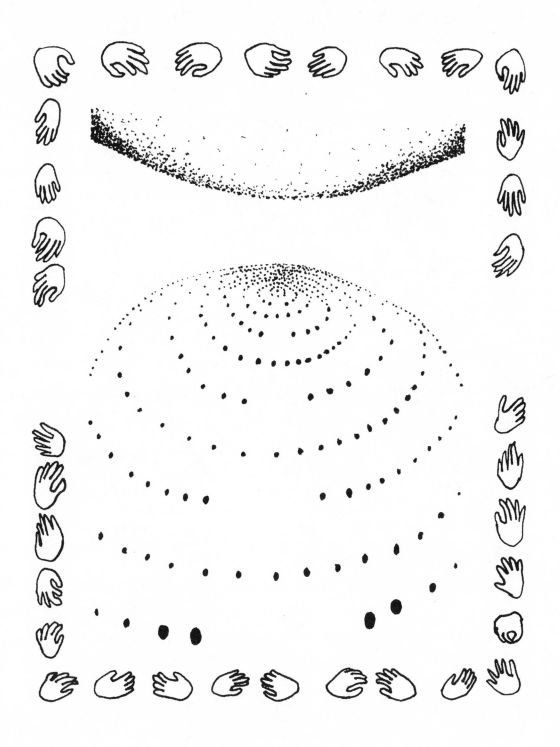

25 Mine Is the Church ("A Dazzling Bouquet")

With a Cajun swing feel, or boogie woogie

Refrain: Mine is the church where ev-ery-bo-dy's wel-come.
1 Come here, all you six - foot glad - i - o - las.
2 We don't sim - ply tol - er - ate each oth - er.
3 Our de - mons keep try - ing to di - vide us;

I know it's true 'cause I got through the door.
Come, all you pur - ple li - lacs shin - ing bright.
We ask and tell, we don't just turn a - way.
They doc - u - ment their lies to make them true.

We are a dazz - ling bou - quet of ev-ery kind of flow - er
Come, let us all bloom to-geth - er in the gar - den:
We give at - ten - tion to ev - ery bud and blos-som.
To - day we're freed from our judg - ing and ex - clud-ing.

Sing refrain at beginning and end.
May also be sung between stanzas.

Jump in the vase, 'cause we've got space for more.
A car - ni - val of fra-grance and de - light.
Let ev - 'ry face come grace the grand bou-quet.
Just look a-round, en - joy the love - ly view.

WORDS AND MUSIC: Bret Hesla, 1995; copyright © 1995 Bret Hesla; admin. by Augsburg Fortress Press.

25 Mine Is the Church ("A Dazzling Bouquet")

Refrain: Mine is the church where everybody's welcome.
I know it's true 'cause I got through the door.
We are a dazzling bouquet of every kind of flower.
Jump in the vase, 'cause we've got space for more.

1 Come here, all you six-foot gladiolas.
Come, all you purple lilacs shining bright.
Come, let us all bloom together in the garden:
A carnival of fragrance and delight.
Refrain

2 We don't simply tolerate each other.
We ask and tell, we don't just turn away.
We give attention to every bud and blossom.
Let ev'ry face come grace the grand bouquet.
Refrain

3 Our demons keep trying to divide us;
They document their lies to make them true.
Today we're freed from our judging and excluding.
Just look around, enjoy the lovely view.
Refrain

Words and Music: Bret Hesla, 1995; copyright © 1995 Bret Hesla; admin. by Augsburg Fortress Press.

26 Mothering God, You Gave Me Birth

1 Moth - er - ing God, you gave me birth
2 Moth - er - ing Christ, you took my form,
3 Moth - er - ing Spir - it, nur - t'ring one,

in the bright morn - ing of this world.
off - er - ing me your food of light,
in arms of pa - tience hold me close,

Cre - a - tor, Source of ev - 'ry breath, you
grain of all life, and fruit of love, your
so that in faith I root and grow un -

are my rain, my wind, my sun.
ver - y bod - y for my peace.
til I flow'r, un - til I know.

WORDS: Jean Wiebe Janzen, 1991, based on the writings of Julian of Norwich;
     copyright © 1991 Jean Wiebe Janzen.
MUSIC: MOTHER ROUND by Jane Ramseyer Miller, 1996; copyright © 1997 The Pilgrim Press.

26 Mothering God, You Gave Me Birth

1   Mothering God, you gave me birth
    in the bright morning of this world.
    Creator, Source of ev'ry breath,
    you are my rain, my wind, my sun.

2   Mothering Christ, you took my form,
    offering me your food of light,
    grain of all life, and fruit of love,
    your very body for my peace.

3   Mothering Spirit, nurt'ring one,
    in arms of patience hold me close,
    so that in faith I root and grow
    until I flow'r, until I know.

WORDS: Jean Wiebe Janzen, 1991, based on the writings of Julian of Norwich;
    copyright © 1991 Jean Wiebe Janzen.
MUSIC: MOTHER ROUND by Jane Ramseyer Miller, 1996;
    copyright © 1997 The Pilgrim Press.

27 My Mother's Life I Celebrate This Day

1 My mother's life I celebrate this day,
2 How like a human mother God gives life
3 God nurtures us in common daily ways,
4 And though a mother's passion is to hold,

for God's light is reflected in her face.
and knits our cells together in the womb.
with warmth and comfort, food and clothes and bread,
her final act of loving lets us go

I thank you, God, for your incarnate love
God knows us well before we know ourselves,
shares knowledge till we understand our world,
to freely claim the life that she has giv'n,

made known to me in human flesh and grace.
gives love before the crib, beyond the tomb.
and wisdom so our ignorance is shed.
find for ourselves the things we need to know.

WORDS: Martha Postlethwaite, 1995; copyright © 1997 The Pilgrim Press.
MUSIC: SURSUM CORDA by Alfred Morton Smith, 1941;
copyright © 1941 Church of the Ascension, Atlantic City, NJ.

27 My Mother's Life I Celebrate This Day

1 My mother's life I celebrate this day,
  for God's light is reflected in her face.
  I thank you, God, for your incarnate love
  made known to me in human flesh and grace.

2 How like a human mother God gives life
  and knits our cells together in the womb.
  God knows us well before we know ourselves,
  gives love before the crib, beyond the tomb.

3 God nurtures us in common daily ways,
  with warmth and comfort, food and clothes and bread,
  shares knowledge till we understand our world,
  and wisdom so our ignorance is shed.

4 And though a mother's passion is to hold,
  her final act of loving lets us go
  to freely claim the life that she has giv'n,
  find for ourselves the things we need to know.

WORDS: Martha Postlethwaite, 1995; copyright © 1997 The Pilgrim Press.
MUSIC: SURSUM CORDA by Alfred Morton Smith, 1941; copyright © 1941
    Church of the Ascension, Atlantic City, NJ.

28 Mystery in Darkness

1 Mys-ter-y in dark-ness, feel the Spir-it's breath.
2 Cat's eyes fa-vor night-fall, sun-set dis-ap-pears,
3 Moth in silk-y cov-'ring, ba-by spi-der's home,
4 Star-fish on the sea-floor, half-moon in the sky.

Praise light's ho-ly ab-sence, grant-ing space for rest.
Owls in mid-night branch-es perch with-out a fear.
Ten-der seeds are sprout-ing un-der rich-est loam.
Mir-ror on the wa-ter, moon's lamp pass-es by.

Sing for those who sleep now, all who dream and sigh,
Sing for those who sleep now, all who dream and sigh,
Sing for those who sleep now, all who dream and sigh,
Sing for those who sleep now, all who dream and sigh,

WORDS: Joan Prefontaine; copyright © 1997 The Pilgrim Press.
MUSIC: Donna Kasbohm, 1996; copyright © 1997 The Pilgrim Press.

Source of ev - 'ry   com - fort,   heal - ing dark,   a - bide.
Source of ev - 'ry   com - fort,   heal - ing dark,   a - bide.
Source of ev - 'ry   com - fort,   heal - ing dark,   a - bide.
Com - fort and   af -   firm us,   heal - ing strength, a -

bide.

28 Mystery in Darkness

1 Mystery in darkness,
   feel the Spirit's breath.
   Praise light's holy absence,
   granting space for rest.
   Sing for those who sleep now,
   all who dream and sigh,
   Source of ev'ry comfort,
   healing dark, abide.

2 Cats' eyes favor nightfall,
   sunset disappears,
   Owls in midnght branches
   perch without a fear.
   Sing for those who sleep now,
   all who dream and sigh,
   Source of ev'ry comfort,
   healing dark, abide.

3 Moth in silky cov'ring,
   baby spider's home,
   Tender seeds are sprouting
   under richest loam.
   Sing for those who sleep now,
   all who dream and sigh,
   Source of ev'ry comfort,
   healing dark, abide.

4 Starfish on the sea-floor,
   half-moon in the sky.
   Mirror on the water,
   moon's lamp passes by.
   Sing for those who sleep now,
   all who dream and sigh,
   Comfort and affirm us,
   healing strength, abide.

WORDS: Joan Prefontaine; copyright © 1997 The Pilgrim Press.
MUSIC: Donna Kasbohm, 1996; copyright © 1997 The Pilgrim Press.

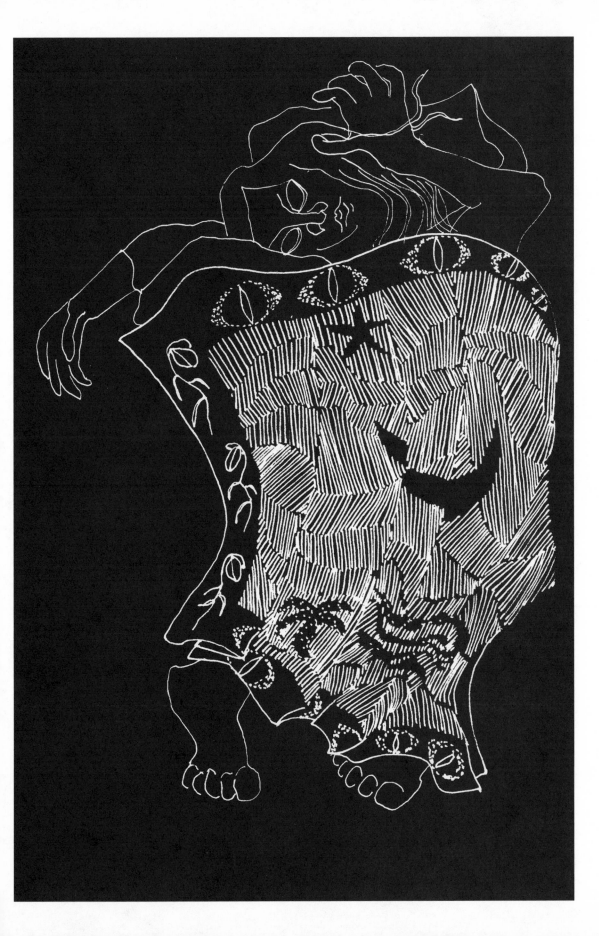

29 Nameless Women, Full of Passion

1 Name-less wom-en, full of pas - sion, flesh and blood and burn - ing soul;
2 Hum - ble wi - dow on a pen - sion, poor by an - y stan - dards set,
3 Wom - an bleed-ing in se - clu - sion suf - fers shame for twelve long years.
4 Name-less wom - en, some-one's moth - er, some-one's sis - ter, teach - er, friend.

Lived their lives in ac - tive wit - ness to the pow'r of love made whole.
Knows the joy of thank-ful giv - ing; trust - ing God, her needs are met.
Trusts that Je - sus' touch will heal her; trans-for - ma - tion dries her tears.
Through their lives of faith - ful jour - ney show us love that has no end.

No - ah's wife whose name is ab - sent sure - ly earns a seat of grace.
Gen - tile wom - an, des - p'rate moth - er, seek - ing for her daugh - ter's cure.
Wom - an bent by years of hard - ship, bear - ing bur - dens, full of care;
We give thanks for name - less wom - en, filled with pas - sion to the core.

Feed - ing crea - tures, clean - ing sta - bles, faith that leads to un - known place.
Shouts till Je - sus sees and hears her, for all peo - ple grace is sure.
Je - sus frees her from her strug - gle; strikes op - pres - sion ev - ery - where.
May our lives bear ac - tive wit - ness to for - get their names no more.

WORDS: Martha Postlethwaite; copyright © 1997 The Pilgrim Press.
MUSIC: BEACH SPRING, attrib. to B. F. White, 1844; harm. *The New Century Hymnal*,
    copyright © 1992 The Pilgrim Press.

29 Nameless Women, Full of Passion

1   Nameless women, full of passion,
    flesh and blood and burning soul;
    Lived their lives in active witness
    to the pow'r of love made whole.
    Noah's wife whose name is absent
    surely earns a seat of grace.
    Feeding creatures, cleaning stables,
    faith that leads to unknown place.

2   Humble widow on a pension,
    poor by any standards set,
    Knows the joy of thankful giving;
    trusting God, her needs are met.
    Gentile woman, desp'rate mother,
    seeking for her daughter's cure.
    Shouts till Jesus sees and hears her,
    for all people grace is sure.

3   Woman bleeding in seclusion
    suffers shame for twelve long years.
    Trusts that Jesus' touch will heal her;
    transformation dries her tears.
    Woman bent by years of hardship,
    bearing burdens, full of care;
    Jesus frees her from her struggle;
    strikes oppression everywhere.

4   Nameless women, someone's mother,
    someone's sister, teacher, friend.
    Through their lives of faithful journey
    show us love that has no end.
    We give thanks for nameless women,
    filled with passion to the core.
    May our lives bear active witness
    to forget their names no more.

WORDS: Martha Postlethwaite; copyright © 1997 The Pilgrim Press.
MUSIC: BEACH SPRING, attrib. to B. F. White, 1844; harm. *The New Century Hymnal*,
   copyright © 1992 The Pilgrim Press.

30 O Falling Water

WORDS: Joan Prefontaine, based on *I, Rigoberta Menchu: An Indian Woman in Guatemala*,
Verso, 1984; copyright © 1997 The Pilgrim Press.
MUSIC: PUES SI VIVIMOS, anon. Mexican folk melody; arr. copyright © 1997 The Pilgrim Press.

30 O Falling Water

1 O falling water, O healing breeze,
   You paint our highland with flow'rs and trees.
   Refrain: Guatemalan earth,
                    Guatemalan sky,
                    We are sun's children;
                    hear our lullaby.

2 O mother earth, out of death's decay,
   Our people rise, white and yellow maize.
   Refrain

3 Grandfather sun, in the heart of sky,
   May your light reach ev'ry evil eye.
   Refrain

4 A few centavos, we earn our way.
   We fight for mem'ries of a future day.
   Refrain

5 Resisting comfort, we appeal each wrong.
   We work and share, compae appeal each
   Refrain

WORDS: Joan Prefontaine, based on *I, Rigoberta Menchu: An Indian Woman in Guatemala*, Verso, 1984;
   copyright © 1997 The Pilgrim Press.
MUSIC: PUES SI VIVIMOS, anon. Mexican folk melody; arr. copyright © 1997 The Pilgrim Press.

31 O Holy Spirit, Root of Life

1 O Holy Spirit, Root of life,
Creator, cleanser of all things,
anoint our wounds, awaken us
with lustrous movement of your wings.

2 Eternal Vigor, Saving One,
you free us by your living Word,
becoming flesh to wear our pain,
and all creation is restored.

3 O Holy Wisdom, Soaring Power,
encompass us with wings unfurled,
and carry us, encircling all,
above, below, and through the world.

WORDS: Jean Wiebe Janzen, 1991, based on the writings of Hildegard of Bingen (12th cent.);
     copyright © 1991 Jean Wiebe Janzen.
MUSIC: PUER NOBIS NASCITUR; Trier manuscript (15th cent.); adapt. Michael Praetorius, 1609;
     harm. George R. Woodward, 1904.

31 O Holy Spirit, Root of Life

1 O Holy Spirit, Root of life,
Creator, cleanser of all things,
anoint our wounds, awaken us
with lustrous movement of your wings.

2 Eternal Vigor, Saving One,
you free us by your living Word,
becoming flesh to wear our pain,
and all creation is restored.

3 O Holy Wisdom, Soaring Power,
encompass us with wings unfurled,
and carry us, encircling all,
above, below, and through the world.

WORDS: Jean Wiebe Janzen, 1991, based on the writings of Hildegard of Bingen (12th cent.);
copyright © 1991 Jean Wiebe Janzen.
MUSIC: PUER NOBIS NASCITUR; Trier manuscript (15th cent.); adapt. Michael Praetorius, 1609;
harm. George R. Woodward, 1904.

32 On the Horizon ("Virgin Ground")

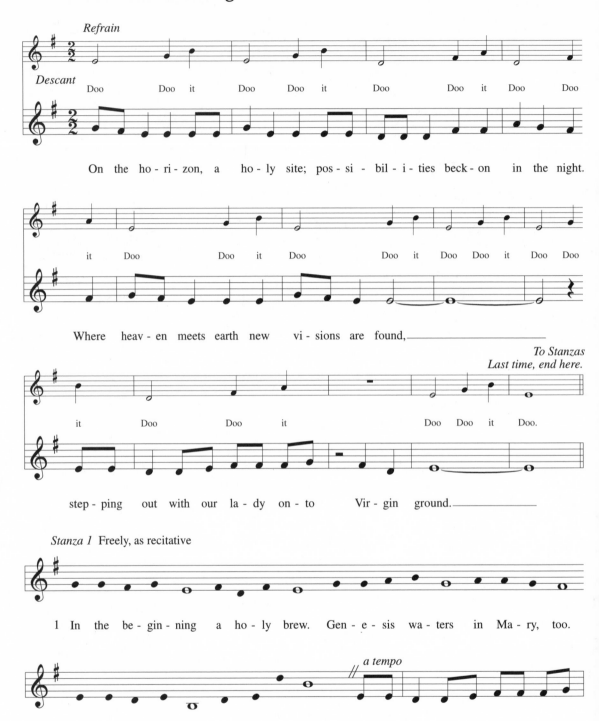

Refrain

Descant

Doo Doo it Doo Doo it Doo Doo it Doo Doo

On the ho - ri - zon, a ho - ly site; pos - si - bil - i - ties beck - on in the night.

it Doo Doo it Doo Doo it Doo Doo it Doo Doo

Where heav - en meets earth new vi - sions are found,_____

To Stanzas
Last time, end here.

it Doo Doo it Doo Doo it Doo.

step - ping out with our la - dy on - to Vir - gin ground._____

Stanza 1 Freely, as recitative

1 In the be - gin - ning a ho - ly brew. Gen - e - sis wa - ters in Ma - ry, too.

a tempo

Hov - er - ing spir - it, "Let there be light!" Step - ping out with our la - dy in - to

WORDS AND MUSIC: Dana McCarthey, 1997; copyright © 1997 The Pilgrim Press.

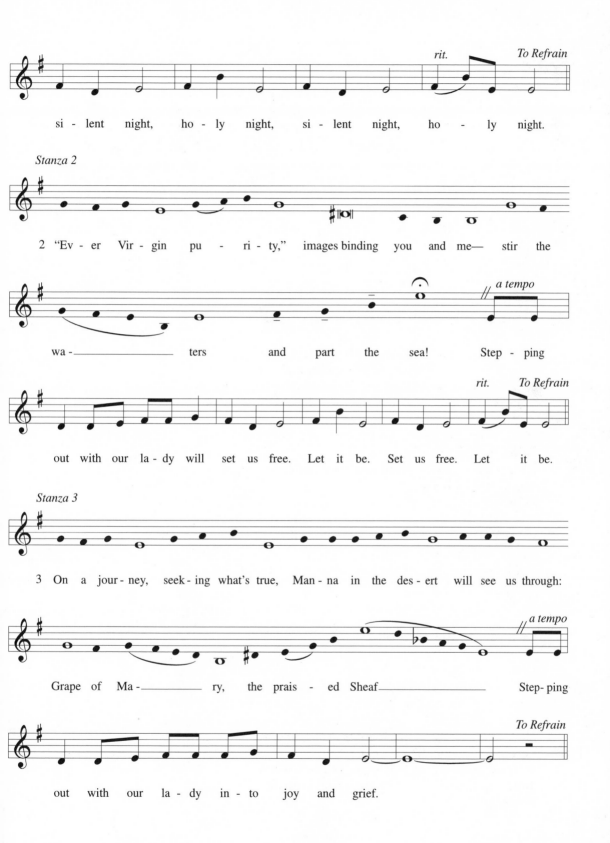

rit.   **To Refrain**

si - lent night, ho - ly night, si - lent night, ho - ly night.

Stanza 2

2 "Ev - er Vir - gin pu – ri - ty," images binding you and me— stir the

a tempo

wa -_____ ters and part the sea! Step - ping

rit.   **To Refrain**

out with our la - dy will set us free. Let it be. Set us free. Let it be.

Stanza 3

3 On a jour - ney, seek - ing what's true, Man - na in the des - ert will see us through:

a tempo

Grape of Ma -_____ ry, the prais - ed Sheaf_____ Step- ping

To Refrain

out with our la - dy in - to joy and grief.

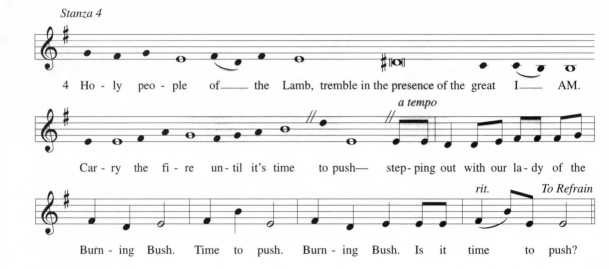

Stanza 4

4 Ho - ly peo - ple of the Lamb, tremble in the presence of the great I AM.

a tempo

Car - ry the fi - re un - til it's time to push— step-ping out with our la - dy of the

rit. *To Refrain*

Burn - ing Bush. Time to push. Burn - ing Bush. Is it time to push?

32 On the Horizon ("Virgin Ground")

Refrain: On the horizon, a holy site;
possibilities beckon in the night.
Where heaven meets earth new visions are found,
stepping out with our lady onto Virgin ground.

1 In the beginning a holy brew. Genesis waters in Mary, too.
Hovering spirit, "Let there be light!"
Stepping out with our lady into silent night, holy night,
silent night, holy night.
Refrain

2 "Ever Virgin purity," images binding you and me—
stir the waters and part the sea!
Stepping out with our lady will set us free. Let it be.
Set us free. Let it be.
Refrain

3 On a journey, seeking what's true,
Manna in the desert will see us through:
Grape of Mary, the praised Sheaf.
Stepping out with our lady into joy and grief.
Refrain

4 Holy people of the Lamb, tremble in the presence of the great I AM.
Carry the fire until it's time to push—
stepping out with our lady of the Burning Bush.
Time to push. Burning Bush. Is it time to push?
Refrain

WORDS AND MUSIC: Dana McCarthey, 1997; copyright © 1997 The Pilgrim Press.

33 Paz, Queremos Paz

Paz, que - re - mos paz, y lib - er - tad en est - e mun - do.

Paz, que - re - mos paz, y lib - er - tad en est - e mun - do.

WORDS AND MUSIC: Traditional, source unknown.

33 Paz, Queremos Paz

Paz, queremos paz,
y libertad en este mundo.
Paz, queremos paz,
y libertad en este mundo.

English translation, not intended to be sung:
"Peace, we want peace and liberty in this world."

WORDS AND MUSIC: Traditional, source unknown.

34 Praise, My Friend, This Holy Cup ("Cup of Blessing")

Deliberate, not fast

1 Praise, my friend, this ho - ly cup, sor - rows
2 Hold up faith - ful - ness and strength, fount of

ov - er - throw - ing. Rocks send forth their
wom - an's bless - ing. Joy is nec - tar

hon - ey streams; hills with milk are flow -
to the soul; truth the heart's con - fess -

WORDS: Joan Prefontaine, 1995; copyright © 1997 The Pilgrim Press.
MUSIC: BLESSING by Madelin Sue Martin, 1995; copyright © 1997 The Pilgrim Press.

ing. Why de - ny the sa - cred feast?
ing. Love turns lips to hon - ey - combs;

Bod - y, chal - ice, tem - ple! Moun - tains drop down
rain - drops en - ter flow - ers. Stead - fast sun and

fresh new wine; God's sup - ply is am - ple.
whirl - ing moon, source of an - cient pow - er.

34 Praise, My Friend, This Holy Cup
("Cup of Blessing")

1 Praise, my friend, this holy cup,
   sorrows overthrowing.
   Rocks send forth their honey streams;
   hills with milk are flowing.
   Why deny the sacred feast?
   Body, chalice, temple!
   Mountains drop down fresh new wine;
   God's supply is ample.

2 Hold up faithfulness and strength,
   fount of woman's blessing.
   Joy is nectar to the soul;
   truth the heart's confessing.
   Love turns lips to honeycombs;
   raindrops enter flowers.
   Steadfast sun and whirling moon,
   source of ancient power.

WORDS: Joan Prefontaine, 1995; copyright © 1997 The Pilgrim Press.
MUSIC: BLESSING by Madelin Sue Martin, 1995; copyright © 1997 The Pilgrim Press.

35 Sanna

"Sanna" is a shortened form of "Hosanna."

WORDS: Traditional.
MUSIC: South African; arr. Geoff Weaver;
copyright © 1993 Hope Publishing Co., Carol Stream, IL 60188.

36 Seeking Healing in Our Journey

Seek- ing heal- ing in our jour - ney we have found com - mu - ni - ty.

May the wa - ter, gift of pro - mise, hearts of love that here sur - round us
May the oil, a gift of pro - mise, hearts of love that here sur - round us
May the bread, a gift of pro - mise, hearts of love that here sur - round us

be a bless - ed rem - e - dy, of - fer life's best en - er - gy.
be a bless - ed rem - e - dy, of - fer life's best en - er - gy.
be a bless - ed rem - e - dy, of - fer life's best en - er - gy.

WORDS: Jane Ramseyer Miller, 1995; copyright © 1997 The Pilgrim Press.
MUSIC: SEEKING HEALING by Jane Ramseyer Miller, 1995; arr. Madelin Sue Martin, 1997;
          copyright © 1997 The Pilgrim Press.

36 Seeking Healing in Our Journey

1 Seeking healing in our journey
   we have found community.
   May the water, gift of promise,
   hearts of love that here surround us
   be a blessed remedy,
   offer life's best energy.

2 Seeking healing in our journey
   we have found community.
   May the oil, a gift of promise,
   hearts of love that here surround us
   be a blessed remedy,
   offer life's best energy.

3 Seeking healing in our journey
   we have found community.
   May the bread, a gift of promise,
   hearts of love that here surround us
   be a blessed remedy,
   offer life's best energy.

WORDS: Jane Ramseyer Miller, 1995; copyright © 1997 The Pilgrim Press.
MUSIC: SEEKING HEALING by Jane Ramseyer Miller, 1995; arr. Madelin Sue Martin, 1997; copyright © 1997 The Pilgrim Press.

37 Si Fui Motivo de Dolor, Oh Dios
(If I Have Been the Source of Pain, O God)

1 Si fui mo-ti-vo de do-lor, oh Dios; si por mi
2 Si va-na y fú-til mi pa-la-bra fue; si al que su-

1 If I have been the source of pain, O God; If to the
2 If I have spo-ken words of cru-el-ty; If I have

cau-sa el dé-bil tro-pe-zó; si en tus ca-mi-nos
frí-a en su do-lor de-jé; no me con-de-nes,

weak I have re-fused my strength; If, in re-bel-lion,
left some suf-fering un-re-lieved; Con-demn not my in-

yo no qui-se an-dar, ¡per-dón, oh Dios!
tú, por mi mal-dad, ¡per-dón, oh Dios!

I have strayed a-way; For-give me, God.
sen-si-ti-vi-ty; For-give me, God.

(Verse 4) A-mén, A- mén.

3 Si por la vi-da qui-se an-dar en paz,
tran-qui-lo, li-bre y sin lu-char por ti
cuan-do an-he-la-bas ver-me en la lid,
¡per-dón, oh Dios!

3 If I've insisted on a peaceful life,
Far from the struggles that the gospel brings,
When you prefer to guide me to the strife,
Forgive me, God.

4 Es-cu-cha oh Dios, mi hu-mil-de con-fe-sión
y lí-bra-me de ten-ta-ción su-til;
pre-ser-va siem-pre mi al-ma en tu re-dil.
A-mén, A-mén.

4 Receive, O God, this ardent word of prayer,
And free me from temptation's subtle snare,
With tender patience, lead me to your care,
Amen, Amen.

WORDS: Sara M. de Hall; English trans. Janet W. May, 1992; copyright © 1992 The Pilgrim Press.
MUSIC: CAMACUA by Pablo D. Sosa; copyright © 1988 Pablo Sosa.

37 Si Fui Motivo de Dolor, Oh Dios
(If I Have Been the Source of Pain, O God)

1 Si fui motivo de dolor, oh Dios;
si por mi causa el débil tropezó;
si en tus caminos yo no quise andar,
¡perdón, oh Dios!

2 Si vana y fútil mi palabra fue;
si al que sufría en su dolor dejé;
no me condenes, tú, por mi maldad,
¡perdón, oh Dios!

3 Si por la vida quise andar en paz,
tranquilo, libre y sin luchar por ti
cuando anhelabas verme en la lid,
¡perdón, oh Dios!

4 Escucha oh Dios, mi humilde confesión
y líbrame de tentación sutil;
preserva siempre mi alma en tu redil.
Amén, Amén.

1 If I have been the source of pain, O God;
If to the weak I have refused my strength;
If, in rebellion, I have strayed away;
Forgive me, God.

2 If I have spoken words of cruelty;
If I have left some suffering unrelieved;
Condemn not my insensitivity;
Forgive me, God.

3 If I've insisted on a peaceful life,
Far from the struggles that the gospel brings,
When you prefer to guide me to the strife,
Forgive me, God.

4 Receive, O God, this ardent word of prayer,
And free me from temptation's subtle snare,
With tender patience, lead me to your care.
Amen, Amen.

WORDS: Sara M. de Hall; English trans. Janet W. May, 1992; copyright © 1992 The Pilgrim Press.
MUSIC: CAMACUA by Pablo D. Sosa; copyright © 1988 Pablo Sosa.

38 Sophia as a Breath of God

1 So - phi - a as a breath of God bends pow-er to a
2 So - phi - a's glo - ry nev - er rests; her crown of peace un -
3 So - phi - a sports up - on the wind to op - en ev - 'ry
4 So - phi - a's voice is mag - ni - fied and ech - oes through the

form: Cre - a - tion washed with stars and mist, the
furls; Her truth ob - scures our eyes like smoke, her
gate. She sent us play - ful - ness for pain and
Word While giv - ing bold and cer - tain hope to

earth with sea and storm. In - spir - ing teach - er,
treas - ure more than pearls. She calls us through our
skills to com - pen - sate. Her scent is cast from
those who've gone un - heard. Like an - cient ol - ive

WORDS: Joan Prefontaine; copyright © 1997 The Pilgrim Press.
MUSIC: SOPHIA by Donna Kasbohm; copyright © 1997 The Pilgrim Press.

mes - sen - ger, she holds an art - ist's wheel. Her
wind - ing streets where Je - sus too is known. She
cin - na - mon, a rose of Jer - i - cho, a -
trees or palms, like vines with spread - ing shoots: "Ap -

col - ors in - ter - sect our sleep, ex - pos - ing what is real.
starts us on a firm - er path and draws us glad - ly home.
ca - cia, in - cense, clouds, and myrrh from love's rich af - ter - glow.
proach, all those de - sir - ing me, and take your fill of fruit."

38 Sophia as a Breath of God

1 Sophia as a breath of God bends power to a form:
Creation washed with stars and mist, the earth with sea and storm.
Inspiring teacher, messenger, she holds an artist's wheel.
Her colors intersect our sleep, exposing what is real.

2 Sophia's glory never rests; her crown of peace unfurls;
Her truth obscures our eyes like smoke, her treasure more than pearls.
She calls us through our winding streets where Jesus too is known.
She starts us on a firmer path and draws us gladly home.

3 Sophia sports upon the wind to open ev'ry gate.
She sent us playfulness for pain and skills to compensate.
Her scent is cast from cinnamon, a rose of Jericho,
Acacia, incense, clouds, and myrrh from love's rich afterglow.

4 Sophia's voice is magnified and echoes through the Word
while giving bold and certain hope to those who've gone unheard.
Like ancient olive trees or palms, like vines with spreading shoots:
"Approach, all those desiring me, and take your fill of fruit."

WORDS: Joan Prefontaine; copyright © 1997 The Pilgrim Press.
MUSIC: SOPHIA by Donna Kasbohm; copyright © 1997 The Pilgrim Press.

39 Sophia, Creator God

Unison

Sophia, Creator God, let your milk and honey flow.

Sophia, Creator God, shower us with your love.

Harmony

Sophia, Creator God, let your milk and honey flow.

Sophia, Creator God, shower us with your love.

Words: Hilda Kuester; copyright © 1997 The Pilgrim Press.
Music: Jeanne Cotter; copyright © 1997 The Pilgrim Press.

39 Sophia, Creator God

Sophia, Creator God,
let your milk and honey flow.
Sophia, Creator God,
shower us with your love.

Words: Hilda Kuester; copyright © 1997 The Pilgrim Press.
Music: Jeanne Cotter; copyright © 1997 The Pilgrim Press.

40 Take the Dark Strength of Our Nights

1 Take the dark strength of our nights, soft with pee — ny wal - lies'* lights.
2 Take the pro - test of our need, what the gar - den? what the weed?
3 Take the is - land's hu - man skills, danc - ing seas and wise old hills.

Take the star - signs wheel - ing round, while the steel drum melts to sound.
Take the orb and break the chain, break the shack - les of the brain.
Take our Je - sus' gen - tle power, call the peo - ple to this hour.

Take and weave a womb of night that we may live, that we may live.
Take and weave a womb of right that we may live, that we may live.
Take and weave a womb of light that we may live, that we may live.

"Peeny wallies" is a Jamaican term for fireflies.

WORDS: John Hoad, 1971; from *Cantate Domino*, copyright © 1980 World Council of Churches.
MUSIC: LINSTEAD, Jamaican folk song; arr. Doreen Potter, 1972;
      copyright © 1975 Hope Publishing Co., Carol Stream, IL 60188.

40 Take the Dark Strength of Our Nights

1 Take the dark strength of our nights,
   soft with peeny wallies'* lights.
   Take the starsigns wheeling round,
   while the steel drum melts to sound.
   Take and weave a womb of night
   that we may live, that we may live.

2 Take the protest of our need,
   what the garden? what the weed?
   Take the orb and break the chain,
   break the shackles of the brain.
   Take and weave a womb of right
   that we may live, that we may live.

3 Take the island's human skills,
   dancing seas and wise old hills.
   Take our Jesus' gentle power,
   call the people to this hour.
   Take and weave a womb of light
   that we may live, that we may live.

*"Peeny wallies" is a Jamaican term for fireflies.

Words: John Hoad, 1971; from *Cantate Domino*, copyright © 1980 World Council of Churches.
Music: LINSTEAD, Jamaican folk song; arr. Doreen Potter, 1972; copyright © 1975
   Hope Publishing Co., Carol Stream, IL 60188.

41 We Are Shadows on the Rock ("Shadows on the Rock")

1 We are shad - ows on the rock, We are chil - dren at our play. We are
2 We are shad - ows on the rock, ev - 'ry col - or, ev - 'ry hue. We are

peo - ple of the earth. We are root - ed in this clay. We are
wo - ven strands of cloth and our strength will see us through. We are

lov - ers of our globe. We are sing - ers of the soul. We are
crea - tures of the air. We are crea - tures of the sea. We are

"our bleed - ing world!"
"to lib - er - ty!"

call - ing young and old, "Come and heal our bleed - ing_____ world!"
call - ing young and old, "Bring our earth to lib - er_____ - ty!"

WORDS AND MUSIC: Jane Ramseyer Miller, 1994; copyright © 1997 The Pilgrim Press.

41 We Are Shadows on the Rock ("Shadows on the Rock")

Soprano descant

Ash - es to ash - es, dust to dust. We are liv - ing crea - tures and

we have seen e - nough! Ash - es to ash - es, dust to dust.

We are liv - ing crea - tures and we have seen e - nough!

"At Hiroshima there is a museum. Outside the museum there is a rock, and on the rock there is a shadow.

The shadow is all that remains of the human being that stood there on August 6th, 1945, when the nuclear age began."

41 We Are Shadows on the Rock ("Shadows on the Rock")

1 We are shadows on the rock,
We are children at our play.
We are people of the earth.
We are rooted in this clay.
We are lovers of our globe.
We are singers of the soul.
We are calling young and old,
"Come and heal our bleeding world!"

2 We are shadows on the rock,
ev'ry color, ev'ry hue.
We are woven strands of cloth
and our strength will see us through.
We are creatures of the air.
We are creatures of the sea.
We are calling young and old,
"Bring our earth to liberty!"

Soprano descant: Ashes to ashes, dust to dust.
We are living creatures and we have seen enough!
Ashes to ashes, dust to dust.
We are living creatures and we have seen enough!

WORDS AND MUSIC: Jane Ramseyer Miller, 1994; copyright © 1997 The Pilgrim Press.

42 We Are Women at the Well ("Women at the Well")

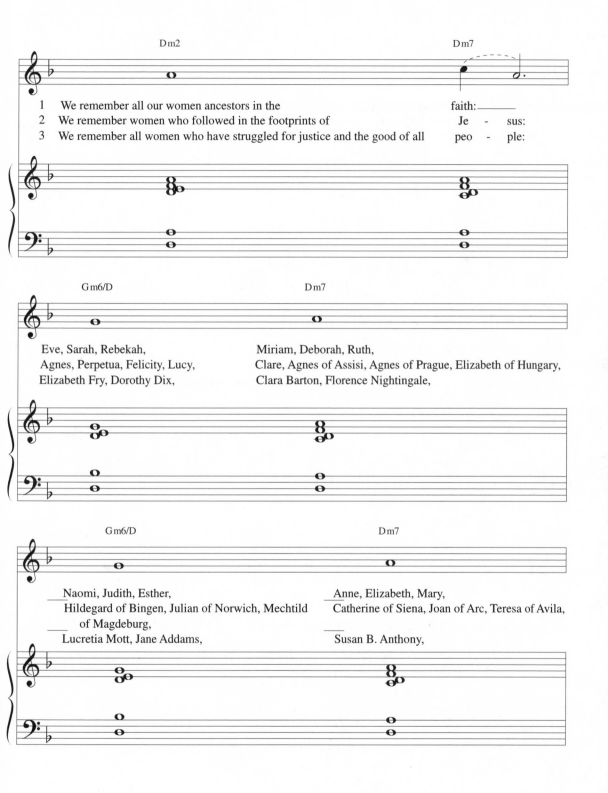

Dm2　　　　　　　　　　　　　　　　　　Dm7

1　We remember all our women ancestors in the　　　　　　faith:_____
2　We remember women who followed in the footprints of　　Je - sus:
3　We remember all women who have struggled for justice and the good of all　peo - ple:

Gm6/D　　　　　　　　　　　　　Dm7

Eve, Sarah, Rebekah,　　　　　　　　　Miriam, Deborah, Ruth,
Agnes, Perpetua, Felicity, Lucy,　　　　Clare, Agnes of Assisi, Agnes of Prague, Elizabeth of Hungary,
Elizabeth Fry, Dorothy Dix,　　　　　　Clara Barton, Florence Nightingale,

Gm6/D　　　　　　　　　　　　　Dm7

____Naomi, Judith, Esther,　　　　　　____Anne, Elizabeth, Mary,
　　Hildegard of Bingen, Julian of Norwich, Mechtild　　Catherine of Siena, Joan of Arc, Teresa of Avila,
____　of Magdeburg,
　　Lucretia Mott, Jane Addams,　　　　　　Susan B. Anthony,

Gm6/D   Dm7

(1) ___ Martha, Mary Magdalene, Anna,   ___ Phoebe, Lydia, Prisca,
(2)   Kateri Tekakwitha, Elizabeth Ann Seton,   Mother Cabrini, Bernadette of Lourdes,
    ___ Thérèse of Lisieux,   ___ Mother Alfred Moes,
(3)   Sojourner Truth, Harriet Tubman,   Rosa Parks, Thea Bowman,

1-2 A   *To Refrain*   3   Gm6/D   Dm7

(1) May we nev-er for-get them!
(2) May we nev-er for-get them!

(3) Dorothy Day, Catherine Doherty,   Ita Ford, Maura Clarke,

3   Gm6/D   Dm7   A   *To Refrain*

Dorothy Kazel, Jean Donovan,   Mother Teresa,   May we nev-er for-get them!

42 We Are Women at the Well ("Women at the Well")

Refrain: We are women at the well,
thirsting for your living water,
bringing you our hearts of longing.
Come and fill us now.
We are women at the well,
thirsting for your living water,
bringing you our hearts of longing.
Come and fill us now.

Litany 1
We remember all our women ancestors in the faith:
Eve, Sarah, Rebekah,
Miriam, Deborah, Ruth,
Naomi, Judith, Esther,
Anne, Elizabeth, Mary,
Martha, Mary Magdalene, Anna,
Phoebe, Lydia, Prisca,
May we never forget them!
Refrain

Litany 2
We remember women who followed in the footprints of Jesus:
Agnes, Perpetua, Felicity, Lucy,
Clare, Agnes of Assisi, Agnes of Prague, Elizabeth of Hungary,
Hildegard of Bingen, Julian of Norwich, Mechtild of Magdeburg,
Catherine of Siena, Joan of Arc, Teresa of Avila,
Kateri Tekakwitha, Elizabeth Ann Seton, Thérèse of Lisieux,
Mother Cabrini, Bernadette of Lourdes, Mother Alfred Moes,
May we never forget them!
Refrain

Litany 3
We remember all the women who have struggled for justice
and the good of all people:
Elizabeth Fry, Dorothy Dix,
Clara Barton, Florence Nightingale,
Lucretia Mott, Jane Addams,
Susan B. Anthony,
Sojourner Truth, Harriet Tubman,
Rosa Parks, Thea Bowman,
Dorothy Day, Catherine Doherty,
Ita Ford, Maura Clarke,
Dorothy Kazel, Jean Donovan, Mother Teresa,
May we never forget them!
Refrain

WORDS AND MUSIC: Cathy Tisel Nelson, from the collection and recording *What You Hold;*
copyright © 1996 Cathy Tisel Nelson, Rochester, MN.

43 We Have Labored ("Weaving a New Creation")

Refrain   Unison

We have la-bored, and we have baked the bread. We have wo-ven cloth, we have nur-tured life. Now we're weav-ing a new cre-a-tion, too.

Last time, end.

Praise, O God, all praise to you!
1 God of sim - ple, com - mon things,
2 As we change our dai - ly lives,
3 Weave our frayed and var - ied strands,
4 Clothed in wis - dom, may we live

God of cloth and bread, help us mend our tat-tered lives. Spir-it be the thread.
jus - tice is our call: saf - er homes and cit - y streets, bread and drink for all.
shap - ing one de - sign. May our col - ors rich - ly blend, as our lives en - twine.
robed in love and praise. May our la - bor turn to joy, as we learn your ways.

Alt. st.4:   Knead us, make us but one loaf, mixed from varied grain.
May our flavors richly blend, foretaste of your reign.

WORDS: Ruth C. Duck, 1993; copyright © 1996 The Pilgrim Press.
MUSIC: RE-IMAGINING by Donna Kasbohm, 1996; copyright © 1997 The Pilgrim Press.

43 We Have Labored ("Weaving a New Creation")

Refrain: We have labored, and we have baked the bread.
We have woven cloth, we have nurtured life.
Now we're weaving a new creation, too.
Praise, O God, all praise to you!

1 God of simple, common things,
God of cloth and bread,
help us mend our tattered lives.
Spirit be the thread.
Refrain

2 As we change our daily lives,
justice is our call:
safer homes and city streets,
bread and drink for all.
Refrain

3 Weave our frayed and varied strands,
shaping one design.
May our colors richly blend,
as our lives entwine.
Refrain

4 Clothed in wisdom, may we live
robed in love and praise,
May our labor turn to joy,
as we learn your ways.
Refrain

Alt. St. 4: Knead us, make us but one loaf,
mixed from varied grain.
May our flavors richly blend,
foretaste of your reign.
Refrain

WORDS: Ruth Duck, 1993; copyright © 1997 The Pilgrim Press.
MUSIC: RE-IMAGINING by Donna Kasbohm, 1996; copyright © 1997 The Pilgrim Press.

44 What You Hold

With strength, legato ♩ = 72

Refrain

What you hold, may you al-ways hold. What you do, may you al-ways do and nev - er a - ban - don, nev-er a-ban-don

To Stanza 1

To Stanza 2

To Stanza 3

WORDS: Based on words of St. Clare of Assisi; trans. Regis Armstrong, OFM,
 Cap., The Franciscan Institute, St. Bonaventure University, St. Bonaventure, NY.
MUSIC: Cathy Tisel Nelson, 1993, from the collection and recording *What You Hold*;
 copyright © 1993 Cathy Tisel Nelson, Rochester, MN.

Freely

3 So that you may offer your vows to the   Most High   in the pursuit of that per -

a tempo ♩ = 72

fection   to which the Spirit of   God   has   called   you,

called   you,   called   you.   *rit.*   *To Refrain*   What you

44 What You Hold

Refrain: What you hold, may you always hold.
What you do, may you always do
and never abandon, never abandon.

1 But with swift pace, light step, unswerving feet,
so that even your steps stir up no dust,
go forward securely, joyfully, and swiftly,
on the path of prudent happiness.
Refrain

2 Believing nothing, agreeing with nothing
that would keep you from this resolution
or that would place a stumbling block for you on the way.
Refrain

3 So that you may offer your vows to the Most High
in the pursuit of that perfection
to which the Spirit of God has called you, called you, called you.
Refrain

WORDS: Based on words of St. Clare of Assisi; trans. Regis Armstrong, OFM, Cap.,
The Franciscan Institute, St. Bonaventure University, St. Bonaventure, NY.
MUSIC: Cathy Tisel Nelson, 1993, from the collection and recording *What You Hold;*
copyright © 1993 Cathy Tisel Nelson, Rochester, MN.

45 When, like the Woman at the Well

Unison

1 When, like the wom-an at the well, I lived with bro-ken dreams,
2 Christ knew my heart, my way-ward ways, yet gave me hope, not fear.
3 I learned I could for-ev-er live and wor-ship God a-right,
4 Each day I lift my cup a-bove, and I a-gain re-ceive
5 Since now I am in grace im-mersed, set free, for-giv-en, whole,

Christ came to me, good news to tell, of ev-er-liv-ing streams.
The God I once thought far a-way, I could ap-proach, draw near.
could trust the pow'r the Spir-it gives to guide me in truth's light.
the liv-ing wa-ter of God's love, re-vealed for my be-lief.
I share with those who are a-thirst the well-springs of my soul!

45 When, like the Woman at the Well

1 When, like the woman at the well,
   I lived with broken dreams,
   Christ came to me, good news to tell,
   of ever-living streams.

2 Christ knew my heart, my wayward ways,
   yet gave me hope, not fear.
   The God I once thought far away,
   I could approach, draw near.

3 I learned I could forever live
   and worship God aright,
   could trust the pow'r the Spirit gives
   to guide me in truth's light.

4 Each day I lift my cup above,
   and I again receive
   the living water of God's love,
   revealed for my belief.

5 Since now I am in grace immersed,
   set free, forgiven, whole,
   I share with those who are a-thirst
   the well-springs of my soul!

WORDS: Edith Sinclair Downing, 1992; copyright © 1998 Selah Publishing Co., Inc.
MUSIC: CRAVEN by Celene Welch, 1992; copyright © 1992 by Hope Publishing Co.,
   Carol Stream, IL 60188.

46 Who Is She?

1 Who is She, nei - ther male nor fe - male, mak - er of all things,
2 Who is She, moth - er - ing her peo - ple, teach - ing them to walk,
3 Who is She, spar - kle in the rap - ids, cool - ness of the well,
4 Why is She, moth - er of all na - ture, long - ing to give birth,

on - ly glimpsed or hint - ed, source of life and gen - der?
lift - ing wea - ry todd - lers, bend - ing down to feed them?
liv - ing power of Je - sus flow - ing from the scrip - tures?
gasp - ing yet ex - ult - ing to a new cre - a - tion?

She is God, moth - er, sis - ter, lov - er; in her love we wake,
She is Love, cry - ing in a sta - ble, teach - ing from a boat,
She is Life, wa - ter, wind, and laugh - ter, calm, yet nev - er still,
She is Hope, nev - er tired of lov - ing, fill - ing all with worth,

WORDS: Brian Wren, 1986; copyright © 1986 Hope Publishing Co., Carol Stream, IL 60188.
MUSIC: Donna Kasbohm, 1996; copyright © 1997 The Pilgrim Press.

move and grow, are daunt - ed, tri - umph and sur - ren - der.
friend - ly with the lep - ers, bound for cru - ci - fix - ion.
swift - ly mov - ing Spir - it, sing - ing in the chang - es.
glad of our a - chiev - ing, lift - ing all to free - dom.

46 Who Is She?

1 Who is She,
   neither male nor female, maker of all things,
   only glimpsed or hinted, source of life and gender?
   She is God,
   mother, sister, lover; in her love we wake,
   move and grow, are daunted, triumph and surrender.

2 Who is She,
   mothering her people, teaching them to walk,
   lifting weary toddlers, bending down to feed them?
   She is Love,
   crying in a stable, teaching from a boat,
   friendly with the lepers, bound for crucifixion.

3 Who is She,
   sparkle in the rapids, coolness of the well,
   living power of Jesus flowing from the scriptures?
   She is Life,
   water, wind and laughter, calm, yet never still,
   swiftly moving Spirit, singing in the changes.

4 Why is She,
   mother of all nature, longing to give birth,
   gasping yet exulting to a new creation?
   She is Hope,
   never tired of loving, filling all with worth,
   glad of our achieving, lifting all to freedom.

WORDS: Brian Wren, 1986; copyright © 1986 Hope Publishing Co., Carol Stream, IL 60188.
MUSIC: Donna B. Kasbohm, 1996; copyright © 1997 The Pilgrim Press.

47 Womb of Life, and Source of Being

1 Womb of life, and source of be - ing, home of ev -
2 Word in flesh, our broth - er Je - sus, born to bring
3 Brood - ing Spir - it, move a - mong us; be our part -
4 Moth - er, Broth - er, ho - ly Part - ner; Fa - ther, Spir -

ery rest - less heart, in your arms the world a -
us sec - ond birth, you have come to stand be -
ner, be our friend. When our mem - ory fails, re -
it, On - ly Son: we would praise your name for -

wak - ened; you have loved us from the start.
side us, know - ing weak - ness, know - ing earth.
mind us whose we are, what we in - tend.
ev - er, one - in - three, and three - in - one.

Words: Ruth C. Duck, 1986, 1990; copyright © 1992 G.I.A. Publications, Inc.
Music: LADUE CHAPEL by Ronald Arnatt; copyright © 1968 Walton Music Corp.

We, your chil - dren, gath - er 'round you, at the ta -
Priest who shares our hu - man strug - gles, Life of Life,
La - bor with us, aid the birth - ing of the new
We would share your life, your pas - sion, share your word

ble you pre - pare. Shar - ing stor - ies, tears, and
and Death of Death, Ris - en Christ, come stand a -
world yet to be, Free of ser - vant, lord, and
of world made new, Ev - er sing - ing, ev - er

laugh - ter, we are nur - tured by your care.
mong us, send the Spir - it by your breath.
mas - ter, free for love and u - ni - ty.
prais - ing, one with all, and one with you.

47 Womb of Life, and Source of Being

1 Womb of life, and source of being,
   home of every restless heart,
   in your arms the world awakened;
   you have loved us from the start.
   We, your children, gather 'round you,
   at the table you prepare.
   Sharing stories, tears, and laughter,
   we are nurtured by your care.

2 Word in flesh, our brother Jesus,
   born to bring us second birth,
   you have come to stand beside us,
   knowing weakness, knowing earth.
   Priest who shares our human struggles,
   Life of Life, and Death of Death,
   Risen Christ, come stand among us,
   send the Spirit by your breath.

3 Brooding Spirit, move among us;
   be our partner, be our friend.
   When our memory fails, remind us
   whose we are, what we intend.
   Labor with us, aid the birthing
   of the new world yet to be,
   Free of servant, lord, and master,
   free for love and unity.

4 Mother, Brother, holy Partner;
   Father, Spirit, Only Son:
   we would praise your name forever,
   one-in-three, and three-in-one.
   We would share your life, your passion,
   share your word of world made new,
   Ever singing, ever praising,
   one with all, and one with you.

Words: Ruth Duck, 1986, 1990; copyright © 1992 G.I.A. Publications, Inc.
Music: LADUE CHAPEL by Ronald Arnatt; copyright © 1968 Walton Music Corp.

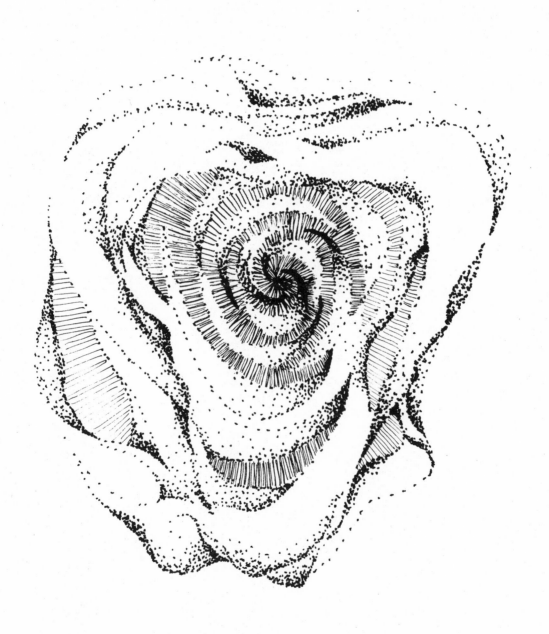

48 Women's Voices, Women's Witness

1 Wom-en's voic-es, wom-en's wit-ness be-ing faith-ful through the years.
2 Wom-en's wit-ness of the ag-es has per-sist-ed through the pain.
3 Tell of vis-its to two wom-en, one a vir-gin, one grown old.
4 Cel-e-brate the faith of An-na and the loy-al-ty of Ruth.
5 When the bread and cup we're shar-ing, when we hold a neigh-bor's hand,

Liv-ing lives of ded-i-ca-tion, find-ing hope a-mid the tears.
Tell the sto-ries of our moth-ers, let us sing their songs a-gain.
Yet to each there came a prom-ise of a gift by God fore-told.
Stand with No-ah and her sis-ters seek-ing jus-tice, speak-ing truth.
Be like Mar-tha in our serv-ice, be like Ma-ry as we learn.

God, you made us in your im-age, from your womb you gave us life.
Wom-en's voic-es of the fu-ture speak of vi-sions yet un-seen.
Tell of one who shared her wa-ter, left re-plen-ished from the well.
Join with us in Sar-ah's laugh-ter, raise your voice in Mir-iam's song.
These our sto-ries that sur-round us, this our her-i-tage to name.

With this life we give you serv-ice. Serve your peo-ple, show your grace.
Tell the sto-ries of our daugh-ters filled with won-der, hope, and dreams.
Tell of wom-en that first East-er to whom Christ said: "Go and tell."
Wom-en's voic-es, wom-en's wit-ness, show-ing wom-en they be-long.
Wom-en's voic-es, wom-en's wit-ness: We re-mem-ber, we pro-claim.

WORDS: Manley Olson, 1996; copyright © 1997 The Pilgrim Press.
MUSIC: HOLY MANNA by William Moore, 1825.

48 Women's Voices, Women's Witness

1 Women's voices, women's witness
  being faithful through the years.
  Living lives of dedication,
  finding hope amid the tears.
  God, you made us in your image,
  from your womb you gave us life.
  With this life we give you service.
  Serve your people, show your grace.

2 Women's witness of the ages
  has persisted through the pain.
  Tell the stories of our mothers,
  let us sing their songs again.
  Women's voices of the future
  speak of visions yet unseen.
  Tell the stories of our daughters
  filled with wonder, hope, and dreams.

3 Tell of visits to two women,
  one a virgin, one grown old.
  Yet to each there came a promise
  of a gift by God foretold.
  Tell of one who shared her water,
  left replenished from the well.
  Tell of women that first Easter
  to whom Christ said: "Go and tell."

4 Celebrate the faith of Anna
  and the loyalty of Ruth.
  Stand with Noah and her sisters
  seeking justice, speaking truth.
  Join with us in Sarah's laughter,
  Raise your voice in Miriam's song.
  Women's voices, women's witness,
  showing women they belong.

5 When the bread and cup we're sharing,
  when we hold a neighbor's hand,
  Be like Martha in our service,
  be like Mary as we learn.
  These our stories that surround us,
  this our heritage to name.
  Women's voices, women's witness:
  We remember, we proclaim.

WORDS: Manley Olson, 1996; copyright © 1997 The Pilgrim Press.
MUSIC: HOLY MANNA by William Moore, 1825.

49 You Call Us ("God, Ecclesia")

Lively

1 You call us to the mar- gins to
(2 You) call us to the cen- ter to
(3 You) call us to each oth- er to
(4 You) call us to the mo- ment to

know those on the edge, to feel their ache for free- dom. You are in em- path- y.
hear the truth with- in, to choose a path that's right- eous. You are in- teg- ri- ty.
seek the wis- dom way, to won- der and to ques- tion. You are com- mu- ni- ty.
in - ter- sect with joy. To find a life of mean- ing. You're syn- chro- ni- ci- ty.

Refrain (divisi)

God, ec- cle- sia, call- ing us by name, Keep- ing us con- nect- ed: the

1 - 3

4

one who makes us whole. 2 You one who makes us whole.
3 You
4 You

WORDS: Nancy J. Berneking, 1996; copyright © 1997 The Pilgrim Press.
MUSIC: GOD, ECCLESIA by Sue Swanson, 1996; copyright © 1997 The Pilgrim Press.

49 You Call Us ("God, Ecclesia")

1 You call us to the margins
to know those on the edge,
to feel their ache for freedom.
You are in empathy.
Refrain: God, ecclesia,
             calling us by name,
             Keeping us connected:
             the one who makes us whole.

2 You call us to the center
to hear the truth within,
to choose a path that's righteous.
You are integrity.
Refrain

3 You call us to each other
to seek the wisdom way,
to wonder and to question.
You are community.
Refrain

4 You call us to the moment
to intersect with joy,
to find a life of meaning.
You're synchronicity.
Refrain

WORDS: Nancy J. Berneking, 1996; copyright © 1997 The Pilgrim Press.
MUSIC: ECCLESIA by Sue Swanson, 1996; copyright © 1997 The Pilgrim Press.

topical index

anointing, 31, 44
birthing, 13, 26
call, 49
care of the earth, 9, 14, 41
community, 5, 33, 36
creation, 28, 31, 38
dance, 7, 9, 10, 24
darkness and light, 28, 40
discipleship, 49
embodiment, 12, 16, 34
empowerment, 15, 34
faithfulness, 1, 2, 20, 29, 34, 48
fire, 15
flowers, 25
forgiveness, 37, 45
God, 19, 38
God's family, 14, 23, 28, 30

grace, 45
healing, 5, 28, 36, 44, 45
hope, 46
images of God, 6, 47
inclusivity, 6, 7, 9, 12, 24, 25, 49
journey, 2, 10, 23, 36, 44
justice, 13
lament, 8
letting go, 27
liberation, 4, 15, 21, 33, 41
mentoring, 10, 18, 21, 49
milk and honey, 2, 39
mother, 19, 27
nurture, 23, 27, 28, 46
passage, 23
perseverance, 4, 44
praise, 12, 13, 18, 35

prophetic vision, 1, 3, 7
relationships, 1
remembrance, 42, 48
resistance, 21, 30, 41
solidarity, 16, 41, 43
Spirit, 1, 11, 13, 16, 28, 31, 46, 47
table, 7, 34
thanksgiving, 35
transformation, 20
Trinity, 26, 47
water, 8, 42, 45, 46
weaving, 40, 43
wholeness, 9, 49
Wisdom, 10, 31
witness, 29, 48
womb, 15, 26, 40, 47
world unity , 24

ritual use index

acclamations, 3, 13, 15, 33, 35, 39
blessing, 2, 3, 4, 7, 9, 13, 15, 34, 36, 42, 44
child/family centered, 9, 14, 18, 23, 30
confession, 37, 45
funerals, 5
gathering, 6, 10, 11, 12, 14, 16, 19, 21, 24, 25, 28, 38, 40, 41, 46, 47, 49
healing service/anointing, 1, 5, 18, 28, 29, 31, 36, 44, 45
intercession, 3, 22, 33, 37, 42
invocation, 3, 11, 16, 19, 37
lamenting, 8, 22, 41
life passage rites, 12, 20, 23

ordination/commission, 1, 18, 38, 42, 44
praise, 12, 13, 14, 18, 35, 47
preaching use, 6
processional, 4, 6, 7, 10, 12, 18, 21, 40, 41, 43
reconciliation, 7, 20, 25
reflection, 15, 19, 20, 26, 27, 30, 44, 46
response to the Word, 4, 8, 15, 26, 27, 29, 31, 38, 42, 45, 46
sending forth, 2, 7, 12, 18, 21, 23, 29, 41, 48
table songs, 7, 34, 43
thanksgiving, 7, 14, 20, 35
unions/weddings, 2, 7, 9

scriptural index

author and composer index

first line index

(song titles shown in italics)